CCNA SECURITY (IINS 210-260)

Exam Practice Questions
Version 2

www.ipspecialist.net

Document Control

Proposal Name	:	CCNA-Security 210-260
Document Version	:	2.0
Document Release Date	:	20-Feb-2019
Reference	:	CCNA-Security-Practice-Questions

Feedback:

If you have any comments regarding the quality of this book, or otherwise alter it to better suit your needs, you can contact us through email at info@ipspecialist.net

Please make sure to include the book title and ISBN in your message

About IPSpecialist

IPSPECIALIST LTD. IS COMMITTED TO EXCELLENCE AND DEDICATED TO YOUR SUCCESS.

Our philosophy is to treat our customers like family. We want you to succeed, and we are willing to do anything possible to help you make it happen. We have the proof to back up our claims. We strive to accelerate billions of careers with great courses, accessibility, and affordability. We believe that continuous learning and knowledge evolution are most important things to keep re-skilling and up-skilling the world.

Planning and creating a specific goal is where IPSpecialist helps. We can create a career track that suits your visions as well as develop the competencies you need to become a professional Network Engineer. We can also assist you with the execution and evaluation of proficiency level based on the career track you choose, as they are customized to fit your specific goals.

We help you STAND OUT from the crowd through our detailed IP training content packages.

Course Features:

❖ Self-Paced learning
  • Learn at your own pace and in your own time
❖ Covers Complete Exam Blueprint
  • Prep-up for the exam with confidence
❖ Case Study Based Learning
  • Relate the content with real life scenarios
❖ Subscriptions that suits you
  • Get more pay less with IPS Subscriptions
❖ Career Advisory Services
  • Let industry experts plan your career journey
❖ Virtual Labs to test your skills
  • With IPS vRacks, you can testify your exam preparations
❖ Practice Questions
  • Practice Questions to measure your preparation standards
❖ On Request Digital Certification
  • On request digital certification from IPSpecialist LTD

About the Authors:

This book has been compiled with the help of multiple professional engineers. These engineers specialize in different fields e.g Networking, Security, Cloud, Big Data, IoT etc. Each engineer develops content in its specialized field that is compiled to form a comprehensive certification guide.

About the Technical Reviewers:

Nouman Ahmed Khan

AWS-Architect, CCDE, CCIEX5 (R&S, SP, Security, DC, Wireless), CISSP, CISA, CISM, Nouman Ahmed Khan is a Solution Architect working with a major telecommunication provider in Qatar. He works with enterprises, mega-projects, and service providers to help them select the best-fit technology solutions. He also works as a consultant to understand customer business processes and helps select an appropriate technology strategy to support business goals. He has more than 14 years of experience working in Pakistan/Middle-East & UK. He holds a Bachelor of Engineering Degree from NED University, Pakistan, and M.Sc. in Computer Networks from the UK.

Abubakar Saeed

Abubakar Saeed has more than twenty-five years of experience, managing, consulting, designing, and implementing large-scale technology projects, extensive experience heading ISP operations, solutions integration, heading Product Development, Pre-sales, and Solution Design. Emphasizing on adhering to Project timelines and delivering as per customer expectations, he always leads the project in the right direction with his innovative ideas and excellent management skills.

Muhammad Yousuf

Muhammad Yousuf is a professional technical content writer. He is Cisco Certified Network Associate in Routing and Switching, holding bachelor's degree in Telecommunication Engineering from Sir Syed University of Engineering and Technology. He has both technical knowledge and industry sounding information, which he uses perfectly in his career.

Sumra Irum Sheikh

Sumra Irum Sheikh is a professional content writer. She worked as Network Security Expert (NSE certified up to level 3), with training in different courses like CCNA cyber security, CCNA Routing and Switching, CCNA security and IT essentials with hands on experience of working with firewalls, routers, switches and other network security tools like alien vault. She holds a bachelor's degree in Telecommunication Engineering from NED University of Engineering and Technology. She has both technical and industrial exposure, which makes her exceptional in research and technical writing.

Free Resources:

Free Resources Include:

Exam Practice Questions in Quiz Simulation: IP Specialists' Practice Questions have been developed keeping in mind the certification exam perspective. The collection of these questions from our technology workbooks is prepared to keep the exam blueprint in mind covering not only important but necessary topics as well. It is an ideal document to practice and revise your certification.

Career Report: This report is a step by step guide for a novice who wants to develop his/her career in the field of computer networks. It answers the following queries:

- Current scenarios and future prospects.
- Is this industry moving towards saturation or are new opportunities knocking at the door?
- What will the monetary benefits be?
- Why to get certified?
- How to plan and when will I complete the certifications if I start today?
- Is there any career track that I can follow to accomplish specialization level?

Furthermore, this guide provides a comprehensive career path towards being a specialist in the field of networking and also highlights the tracks needed to obtain certification.

Our Products

Technology Workbooks

IPSpecialist Technology workbooks are the ideal guides to developing the hands-on skills necessary to pass the exam. Our workbook covers official exam blueprint and explains the technology with real life case study based labs. The content covered in each workbook consists of individually focused technology topics presented in an easy-to-follow, goal-oriented, step-by-step approach. Every scenario features detailed breakdowns and thorough verifications to help you completely understand the task and associated technology.

We extensively used mind maps in our workbooks to visually explain the technology. Our workbooks have become a widely used tool to learn and remember the information effectively.

vRacks

Our highly scalable and innovative virtualized lab platforms let you practice the IP Specialist Technology Workbook at your own time and your own place as per your convenience.

Quick Reference Sheets

Our quick reference sheets are a concise bundling of condensed notes of the complete exam blueprint. It's an ideal handy document to help you remember the most important technology concepts related to certification exam.

Practice Questions

IP Specialists' Practice Questions are dedicatedly designed for certification exam perspective. The collection of these questions from our technology workbooks are prepared to keep the exam blueprint in mind covering not only important but necessary topics as well. It's an ideal document to practice and revise your certification.

Cisco Certifications

Cisco Systems, Inc. is a global technology leader, specializing in networking and communications products and services. The company is probably best known for its business routing and switching products, which direct data, voice and video traffic across networks around the world.

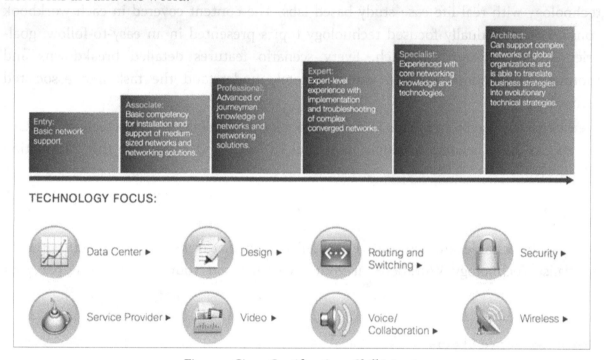

Figure 1 Cisco Certifications Skill Matrix

Cisco offers one of the most comprehensive vendor-specific certification programs in the world. The Cisco Career Certification program begins at the Entry level, then advances to Associate, Professional and Expert levels, and (for some certifications) caps things off at the Architect level.

How does Cisco certifications help?

Cisco certifications are a de facto standard in networking industry help you boost your career in the following ways,

1. Gets your foot in the door
2. Screen job applicants
3. Validate the technical skills of the candidate
4. Ensure quality, competency, and relevancy
5. Improves organization credibility and customer's loyalty
6. Required to maintain organization partnership level with OEMs
7. Helps in Job retention and promotion

Cisco Certification Tracks

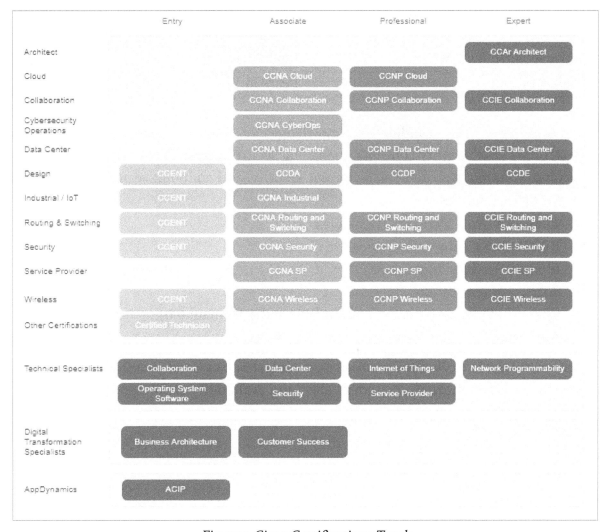

Figure 2 Cisco Certifications Track

About CCNA Security Exam

Cisco Certified Network Associate Security (CCNA Security) validates associate-level knowledge and skills required to secure Cisco networks. With a CCNA Security certification, a network professional demonstrates the skills required to develop a security infrastructure, recognize threats and vulnerabilities to networks, and mitigate security threats. The CCNA Security curriculum emphasizes core security technologies, the installation, troubleshooting and monitoring of network devices to maintain integrity, confidentiality and availability of data and devices, and competency in the technologies that Cisco uses in its security structure.

Exam Number:	210-260 IINS
Associated Certifications:	CCNA Security
Duration:	90 minutes (60-70 questions)
Available Languages:	English, Japanese
Registration:	Pearson VUE

This exam tests the candidate's knowledge of secure network infrastructure, understanding core security concepts, managing secure access, VPN encryption, firewalls, intrusion prevention, web and email content security, and endpoint security using:

- ✓ SIEM Technology
- ✓ Cloud & Virtual Network Topologies
- ✓ BYOD, Bring Your Own Device
- ✓ Identity Services Engine (ISE)
- ✓ 802.1x Authentication
- ✓ Cisco FirePOWER Next Generation IPS (under Domain 6.0)
- ✓ Anti-Malware/Cisco Advanced Malware Protection

This exam validates skills for installation, troubleshooting, and monitoring of a secure network to maintain integrity, confidentiality, and availability of data and devices

Practice Questions

1. Which of the following two next-generation encryption algorithms are recommended by Cisco? (Choose any two.)

   A. 3DES

   B. DES

   C. AES

   D. MD5

   E. SHA-384

2. Which of the following three protocols should the default ACL allow on an access port to enable wired BYOD devices to supply authenticated credentials and connect to the network? (Choose any three.)

   A. MAB

   B. DNS

   C. BOOTP

   D. TFTP

   E. HTTP

   F. 802.1x

3. Which of the following three are the services of cloud networks? (Choose any three)

   A. Software as a Service

   B. Infrastructure as a Service

   C. Platform as a Service

   D. Security as a Service

   E. Compute as a Service

4. In which of the following two situations out-of-band management will be used? (Choose any two.)

   A. when management applications need concurrent access to the device

B. when you require administrator access from multiple locations

C. when a network device fails to forward packets

D. when you require ROMMON access

E. when the control plane fails to respond

5. In which of the following three ways does the TACACS protocol is different from RADIUS? (Choose any three.)

A. TACACS causes fewer packets to be transmitted.

B. TACACS uses TCP to communicate with the Network Access Server (NAS).

C. TACACS can encrypt the entire packet that is sent to the Network Access Server (NAS).

D. TACACS supports per-command authorization.

E. TACACS uses UDP to communicate with the NAS.

F. TACACS encrypts only the password field in an authentication packet.

6. Which of the following two authentication types does OSPF support? (Choose any two.)

A. HMAC

B. AES 256

C. plaintext or clear text

D. MD5

E. SHA-1

F. DES

7. Which of the following two features does CoPP and CPPr use to secure the control plane? (Choose any two.)

A. access lists

B. policy maps

C. class maps

D. QoS

E. traffic classification

F. Cisco Express Forwarding

8. Which of the following two are the characteristics of stateless firewalls are true? (Choose any two.)

   A. They compare the 5-tuple (source IP address/port number, destination IP address/port number and the protocol in use) of each incoming packet against configurable rules.

   B. They cannot track connections.

   C. They are designed to work most efficiently with stateless protocols such as HTTP or HTTPS.

   D. Cisco IOS cannot implement them because the platform is stateful by nature.

   E. The Cisco ASA is implicitly stateless because it blocks all traffic by default.

9. Which of the following three ESP fields can be encrypted during transmission? (Choose any three.)

   A. Security Parameter Index

   B. Sequence Number

   C. MAC Address

   D. Padding

   E. Pad Length

   F. Next Header

10. Which of the following two are the default Cisco IOS privilege levels? (Choose any two.)

    A. 0

    B. 1

    C. 5

    D. 7

    E. 10

    F. 15

11. Which of the following action would the IPS take to prevent an attack from

spreading, whenever an IPS detects an attack?

A. Perform a Layer 6 reset.

B. Deny the connection inline.

C. Deploy an antimalware system.

D. Enable bypass mode.

12. In disk encryption, what is an advantage of implementing a Trusted Platform Module?

A. It can protect against single points of failure.

B. It provides hardware authentication.

C. It supports a more complex encryption algorithm than other disk-encryption technologies.

D. It allows the hard disk to be transferred to another device without requiring re-encryption.

13. Which one of the following is the characteristic of the Integrity component of the CIA triad?

A. to make sure that only authorized parties can manipulate data

B. to determine whether data is relevant

C. to create a process for accessing data

D. to ensure that only authorized parties can view data

14. Which type of secure connectivity does an extranet provide?

A. Provides remote branch offices to your company network

B. Take your company's network to the Internet

C. Provides other company networks to your company network

D. Adds new networks to your company network

15. Which of the following three are the characteristics of host-based IPS? (Choose any three.)

A. It can be deployed at the perimeter.

B. It uses signature-based policies.

C. It works with deployed firewalls.

D. It can generate alerts based on behavior at the desktop level.

E. It can have more restrictive policies than network-based IPS.

F. It can view encrypted files.

16. Which of the following three actions are the limitations when running IPS in promiscuous mode? (Choose any three.)

A. request block connection

B. request block host

C. reset TCP connection

D. deny attacker

E. deny packet

F. modify packet

17. What type of algorithm uses the same key to encrypt and decrypt data?

A. an asymmetric algorithm

B. Public Key Infrastructure algorithm

C. symmetric algorithm

D. IP security algorithm

18. How does the Cisco ASA use Active Directory to authorize VPN users?

A. It sends the username and password to retrieve an ACCEPT or REJECT message from the Active Directory server.

B. It queries the Active Directory server for a specific attribute for the specified user.

C. It redirects requests to the Active Directory server defined for the VPN group.

D. It downloads and stores the Active Directory database to query for future authorization requests.

19. Which one of the following tool an attacker can use to attempt a DDoS attack?

A. Trojan horse

B. Botnet

C. adware

D. virus

20. Which one of the following is the type of security support provided by the Open Web Application Security Project?

A. A Web site security framework.

B. A security discussion forum for Web site developers.

C. Scoring of common vulnerabilities and exposures.

D. Education about common Web site vulnerabilities.

21. Which one of the following attack is the type of Stuxnet virus?

A. hacktivism

B. botnet

C. cyber warfare

D. social engineering

22. Refer to the exhibit.

```
Authentication event fail action next-method
Authentication event no-response action authorize vlan 101
Authentication order mab dot1x webauth
Authentication priority dot1x mab
Authentication port-control auto
Dot1x pae authentication
```

How would the switch respond, if a supplicant enters incorrect credentials for all authentication methods configured on the switch?

A. The switch will cycle through the configured authentication methods indefinitely.

B. The authentication attempt will time out and the switch will place the port into the unauthorized state.

C. The authentication attempt will time out and the switch will place the port into VLAN 101.

D. The supplicant will fail to advance beyond the webauth method.

23. Refer to the exhibit.

```
R1#show snmp
Chassis: FTX123456789
0 SNMP packets input
    6 Bad SNMP version errors
    3 Unknown community name
    9 illegal operation for community name supplied
    4 Encoding errors
    2 Number of requested variables
    0 Number of altered variables
    98 Get-request PDUs
    12 Set-request PDUs
    0 Input queue packet drops (Maximum queue size 1000)
0 SNMP packets output
    0 Too big errors (maximum packet size 1500)
    0 No such name errors
    0 Bad values errors
    0 General errors
    31 Response PDUs
    1 Trap PDUs
```

According to the exhibit above, does how many times was the read-only string used to attempt a write operation?

A. 6

B. 4

C. 9

D. 3

E. 2

24. Refer to the exhibit.

```
R1> show clock detail
.22:22:35>123 UTC Teu Feb 26 2018
Time source is NTP
```

Which of the following statement about the device time is true?

A. The time is authoritative because the clock is in sync.

B. The clock is out of sync.

C. The time is authoritative, but the NTP process has lost contact with its servers.

D. NTP is configured incorrectly.

E. The time is not authoritative.

25. Which of the following statement is true about Cisco ACS authentication and authorization?

A. ACS can query multiple Active Directory domains.

B. ACS uses TACACS to proxy other authentication servers.

C. ACS servers can be clustered to provide scalability.

D. ACS can use only one authorization profile to allow or deny requests.

26. Which of the following VPN feature allows Internet traffic and local LAN/WAN traffic to use the same network connection?

A. hairpinning

B. tunnel mode

C. split tunneling

D. transparent mode

27. Refer to the exhibit given below:

> Crypto ikev1 policy 1
> Encryption aes
> Hash md5
> Authentication pre-share
> Group 2
> Lifetime 14400

What is the purpose of the given command sequence?

A. It configures a site-to-site VPN tunnel.

B. It configures IPSec Phase 2.

C. It configures a crypto policy with a key size of 14400.

D. It configures IKE Phase 1.

28. Which of the following EXTENSIBLE AUTHENTICATION PROTOCOL (EAP) method uses Protected Access Credentials?

A. EAP-PEAP

B. EAP-FAST

C. EAP-GTC

D. EAP-TLS

29. What one of the following is the requirement for locking a wired or wireless device from ISE?

A. The device must be connected to the network when the lock command is executed.

B. The ISE agent must be installed on the device.

C. The organization must implement an acceptable use policy allowing device locking.

D. The user must approve the locking action.

30. Refer to the exhibit, shown below:

> Username HelpDesk privilege 9 password 0 helpdesk
> Username Monitor privilege 8 password 0 watcher
> Username Admin password checkme
> Username Admin privilege 6 autocommand show running
> Privilege exec level 6 configure terminal

According to the exhibit, the Admin user is unable to enter configuration mode on a device with the given sequence of configuration. What changes should be done to the configuration to encounter this problem?

A. Remove the two Username Admin lines.

B. Remove the Privilege exec line.

C. Remove the autocommand keyword and arguments from the Username Admin privilege line.

D. Change the Privilege exec level value to 15.

31. When you reload a router, you issue the dir command to verify the installation and observe that the image file appears to be missing. Which of the following could be the reason that the image file fails to appear in the dir output?

A. The reload command was issued from ROMMON.

B. The secure boot-comfit command is configured.

C. The confreg 0x24 command is configured.

D. The secure boot-image command is configured.

32. Which of the following VPN feature allows traffic to exit the security appliance through the same interface it entered?

A. Split tunneling

B. Hairpinning

C. NAT traversal

D. NAT

33. Refer to the exhibit, given below:

> Crypto map mymap 20 match address 201
> Access-list 201 permit ip 10.10.10.0 255.255.255.0 10.100.100.0 255.255.255.0

What one the following is the result of the given command sequence?

    A. It defines IPSec policy for traffic sourced from 10.100.100.0/24 with a destination of 10.10.10.0/24.

    B. It defines IKE policy for traffic sourced from 10.100.100.0/24 with a destination of 10.10.10.0/24.

    C. It defines IKE policy for traffic sourced from 10.10.10.0/24 with a destination of 10.100.100.0/24.

    D. It defines IPSec policy for traffic sourced from 10.10.10.0/24 with a destination of 10.100.100.0/24.

34. Refer to the exhibit, given below:

Dst	src	state	conn-id	slot
10.10.10.2	10.1.1.5	QM_IDLE	1	0

During the troubleshooting of site-to-site VPN, you issued the "show crypto isakmp sa" command. What does the output above represent?

    A. IPSec Phase 2 is established between 10.10.10.2 and 10.1.1.5.

    B. IPSec Phase 1 is established between 10.10.10.2 and 10.1.1.5.

    C. IPSec Phase 1 is down due to a QM_IDLE state.

    D. IPSec Phase 2 is down due to a QM_IDLE state.

35. Refer to the exhibit, given below:

```
Current peer: 10.1.1.5
PERMIT, Flags={origin_is_acl,}
#pkts encaps: 1205,  #pkts encrypt: 1205,  #pkts digest 1205
#pkts decaps: 1168,  #pkts encrypt: 1168,  #pkts digest 1168
#pkts compressed: 0,  #pkts decompressed: 0
#pkts not compressed: 0,  #pkts compr. failed: 0,
#pkts decompress failed: 0,  #send errors 0, #recv errors 0
Local crypto endpt.: 10.1.1.1, remote crypto endpt.: 10.1.1.5
```

During the troubleshooting of site-to-site VPN, you issued the "show crypto ipsec sa" command. What does the given output represent?

A. ISAKMP security associations are established between 10.1.1.5 and 10.1.1.1.

B. IPSec Phase 2 is established between 10.1.1.1 and 10.1.1.5.

C. IKE version 2 security associations are established between 10.1.1.1 and 10.1.1.5.

D. IPSec Phase 2 is down due to a mismatch between encrypted and decrypted packets.

36. What purpose does the command "send-lifetime local 23:59:00 31 December 31 2013 infinite" serves?

A. It configures the device to begin transmitting the authentication key to other devices at 00:00:00 local time on January 1, 2014 and continue using the key indefinitely.

B. It configures the device to begin accepting the authentication key from other devices immediately and stop accepting the key at 23:59:00 local time on December 31, 2013.

C. It configures the device to generate a new authentication key and transmit it to other devices at 23:59:00 local time on December 31, 2013.

D. It configures the device to begin transmitting the authentication key to other devices at 23:59:00 local time on December 31, 2013 and continue using the key indefinitely.

E. It configures the device to begin accepting the authentication key from other devices at 23:59:00 local time on December 31, 2013 and continue accepting the

key indefinitely.

F. It configures the device to begin accepting the authentication key from other devices at 00:00:00 local time on January 1, 2014 and continue accepting the key indefinitely.

37. What of the following type of packet creates and performs network operations on a network device?

A. data plane packets

B. management plane packets

C. control plane packets

D. services plane packets

38. What might be the results if an attacker installs a rogue switch in a network that sends superior BPDUs?

A. The switch could become the root bridge.

B. The switch could offer fake DHCP addresses.

C. The switch could become a transparent bridge.

D. The switch could be allowed to join the VTP domain.

39. In which one of the following types of attack does an attacker virtually change a device's MAC address and mask the device's true identity?

A. MAC spoofing

B. gratuitous ARP

C. ARP poisoning

D. IP spoofing

40. Which one the following command is used to verify the binding table status?

A. show ip dhcp snooping binding

B. show ip dhcp snooping statistics

C. show ip dhcp snooping database

D. show ip dhcp pool E.show ip dhcp source binding

E. show ip dhcp snooping

41. For what reason does an organization deploy a personal firewall?

A. To determine whether a host meets minimum security posture requirements.

B. To create a separate, non-persistent virtual environment that can be destroyed after a session.

C. To protect endpoints such as desktops from malicious activity.

D. To protect one virtual network segment from another.

E. To protect the network from DoS and syn-flood attacks.

42. Which of the following statement is true about personal firewalls?

A. They are resilient against kernel attacks.

B. They can protect email messages and private documents in a similar way to a VPN.

C. They can protect the network against attacks.

D. They can protect a system by denying probing requests.

43. Which of the following mechanism goes directly into a blocked state, if a switch receives a superior BPDU?

A. Ether Channel guard

B. loop guard

C. root guard

D. BPDU guard

44. Which of the following statement is true about a PVLAN isolated port configured on a switch?

A. The isolated port can communicate with other isolated ports and the promiscuous port.

B. The isolated port can communicate only with the promiscuous port.

C. The isolated port can communicate only with other isolated ports.

D. The isolated port can communicate only with community ports.

45. What happens if an attacker attempts a double tagging attack, if you change the native VLAN on the trunk port to an unused VLAN other than VLAN 1?

   A. A VLAN hopping attack would be prevented.

   B. The attacked VLAN will be pruned.

   C. The trunk port would go into an error-disabled state.

   D. A VLAN hopping attack would be successful.

46. Refer to the exhibit, given below:

> UDP outside 209.165.201.225:53 inside   10.0.0.10:52464,   idle 0:00:01, bytes 266,   flags-

What of the following type of firewall would use the given configuration line?

   A. A Personal Firewall

   B. A Proxy Firewall

   C. A Stateful Firewall

   D. An Application Firewall

   E. A Stateless Firewall

47. Which one is the only permitted operation on zone-based firewalls for processing multicast traffic?

   A. Stateful inspection of multicast traffic is supported only for the self-zone.

   B. Stateful inspection for multicast traffic is supported only between the self-zone and the internal zone.

   C. A control plane policing can protect the control plane against multicast traffic.

   D. Stateful inspection of multicast traffic is supported only for the internal zone.

48. How the traffic between interfaces of the same zone is handled by zone-based firewall?

A. Traffic between interfaces in the same zone is blocked unless you configure the same-security permit command.

B. Traffic between two interfaces in the same zone is allowed by default.

C. Traffic between interfaces in the same zone is blocked unless you apply a service policy to the zone pair.

D. Traffic between interfaces in the same zone is always blocked.

49. Which of the following two statements are true about Telnet access to the ASA? (Choose any two).

A. You must configure an AAA server to enable Telnet.

B. You can access all interfaces on an ASA using Telnet.

C. You must use the command virtual telnet to enable Telnet.

D. You may set VPN to the lowest security interface to telnet an inside interface.

E. Best practice is to disable Telnet and use SSH.

50. Which of the following statement is true about communication over failover interfaces?

A. All information that is sent over the failover interface is sent as clear text, but the stateful failover link is encrypted by default.

B. All information that is sent over the failover and stateful failover interfaces is encrypted by default.

C. All information that is sent over the failover and stateful failover interfaces is sent as clear text by default.

D. User names, passwords, and pre-shared keys are encrypted by default when they are sent over the failover and stateful failover interfaces, but other information is sent as clear text.

51. How does the ASA handle the packet, if a packet matches more than one class map in an individual feature type's policy map?

A. The ASA will apply the actions from only the first matching class map it finds for the feature type. --

B. The ASA will apply the actions from only the last matching class map it finds for the feature type.

C. The ASA will apply the actions from only the most specific matching class map it finds for the feature type.

D. The ASA will apply the actions from all matching class maps it finds for the feature type.

52. For which of the following reason organizations configure multiple security contexts on the ASA firewall?

A. To provide redundancy and high availability within the organization.

B. To enable the use of multicast routing and QoS through the firewall.

C. To separate different departments and business units.

D. To enable the use of VRFs on routers that are adjacently connected.

53. For which one of the following advantage Organizations place an IPS on the inside of a network?

A. It receives traffic that has already been filtered.

B. It can provide higher throughput.

C. It receives every inbound packet.

D. It can provide greater security.

54. What purpose does the FirePOWER impact flag serve?

A. A value that the administrator assigns to each signature.

B. A value that sets the priority of a signature.

C. A value that indicates the potential severity of an attack.

D. A value that measures the application awareness.

55. Which of the following FirePOWER preprocessor engine is used to prevent SYN attacks?

A. Portscan Detection

B. Rate-Based Prevention

C. IP Defragmentation

D. Inline Normalization

56. Which one of the following Sourcefire logging action would you choose to record the most detail about a connection?

A. Enable alerts via SNMP to log events off-box.

B. Enable eStreamer to log events off-box.

C. Enable logging at the end of the session.

D. Enable logging at the beginning of the session.

57. What of the following feature can the SMTP preprocessor in FirePOWER normalize?

A. It can look up the email sender.

B. It compares known threats to the email sender.

C. It can extract and decode email attachments in client to server traffic.

D. It can forward the SMTP traffic to an email filter server.

E. It uses the Traffic Anomaly Detector.

58. Which of the following two solutions can you choose, if you want to allow all of your company's users to access the Internet without allowing other Web servers to collect the IP addresses of individual users? (Choose any two).

A. Configure a proxy server to hide users' local IP addresses.

B. Configure a firewall to use Port Address Translation.

C. Assign unique IP addresses to all users.

D. Assign the same IP address to all users.

E. Install a Web content filter to hide users' local IP addresses.

59. Consider a scenario where a user calls and is not able to access a certain IP address. You have implemented a Sourcefire IPS and configured it to block certain addresses utilizing Security Intelligence IP Address Reputation. What action can you take to allow the user access to the IP address?

A. Create a network based access control rule to allow the traffic.

B. Create a rule to bypass inspection to allow the traffic.

C. Create a whitelist and add the appropriate IP address to allow the traffic.

D. Create a custom blacklist to allow the traffic.

E. Create a user based access control rule to allow the traffic.

60. When one of the following is supposed to be the best time to perform an anti-virus signature update?

A. When the local scanner has detected a new virus.

B. When a new virus is discovered in the wild.

C. When the system detects a browser hook.

D. Every time a new update is available.

61. Which of the following statement is true about application blocking?

A. It blocks access to files with specific extensions.

B. It blocks access to specific network addresses.

C. It blocks access to specific programs.

D. It blocks access to specific network services.

62. What action would you take to block users from accidentally visiting the URL and becoming infected with malware if a specific URL has been identified as containing malware?

A. Enable URL filtering on the perimeter firewall and add the URLs you want to allow to the router's local URL list.

B. Enable URL filtering on the perimeter router and add the URLs you want to allow to the firewall's local URL list.

C. Create a blacklist that contains the URL you want to block and activate the blacklist on the perimeter router.

D. Enable URL filtering on the perimeter router and add the URLs you want to block to the router's local URL list.

E. Create a whitelist that contains the URLs you want to allow and activate the whitelist on the perimeter router.

63. Which of the following three features can protect the data plane? (Choose three.)

A. QoS

B. DHCP-snooping

C. Anti-spoofing

D. ACLs

E. policing

F. IPS

64. In How many numbers can you apply crypto map sets to a router interface?

   A. 4

   B. 1

   C. 3

   D. 2

65. Which of the following represents the correct transition order of STP states on a Layer 2 switch interface?

   A. blocking, listening, learning, forwarding, disabled

   B. listening, learning, blocking, forwarding, disabled

   C. forwarding, listening, learning, blocking, disabled

   D. listening, blocking, learning, forwarding, disabled

66. What is the effect on the company's business, when a company puts a security policy in place?

   A. Minimizing total cost of ownership

   B. Minimizing liability

   C. Minimizing risk

   D. Maximizing compliance

67. Which of the following wildcard mask is associated with a subnet mask of /27?

   A. 0.0.027

   B. 0.0.0.224

   C. 0.0.0.31

   D. 0.0.0.255

68. Which of the following statements are true about reflexive access lists? (Choose any three.)

    A. Reflexive access lists support UDP sessions.

    B. Reflexive access lists support TCP sessions

    C. Reflexive access lists can be attached to extended named IP ACLs

    D. Reflexive access lists create a permanent ACE

    E. Reflexive access lists approximate session filtering using the established keyword Reflexive access lists can be attached to standard named IP ACLs

69. Which three of the following actions can a promiscuous IPS take to mitigate an attack? (Choose any three.)

    A. Modifying packets

    B. Resetting the TCP connection

    C. Requesting host blocking

    D. Requesting connection blocking

    E. Denying packets

    F. Denying frames

70. Which of the following Cisco Security Manager application collects information about device status and uses it to generate notifications and alerts?

    A. FlexConfig

    B. Health and Performance Monitor

    C. Report Manager

    D. Device Manager

71. Which two of the following accounting notices are used to send a failed authentication attempt record to a AAA server? (Choose any two.)

    A. stop-record

    B. start-stop

    C. stop-only

D. stop

72. Which of the following command is used to enable SSH support on a Cisco Router?
    A. crypto key lock rsa
    B. crypto key zeroize rsa
    C. crypto key generate rsa
    D. crypto key unlock rsa

73. Which of the following protocol provides security to Secure Copy?
    A. IPsec
    B. HTTPS
    C. SSH
    D. ESP
    E. SCP

74. Which of the following security zone is automatically defined by the system?
    A. The source zone
    B. The destination zone
    C. The self-zone
    D. The inside zone

75. What purpose does Internet Key Exchange in an IPsec VPN serves? (Choose any two.)
    A. The Internet Key Exchange protocol provides data confidentiality
    B. The Internet Key Exchange protocol provides replay detection
    C. The Internet Key Exchange protocol establishes security associations
    D. The Internet Key Exchange protocol is responsible for mutual authentication

76. Which of the following address block is reserved for locally assigned unique local addresses?
    A. 2002::/16

B. 2001::/32

C. FD00::/8

D. FB00::/8

77. For which of the following reason the error message Router(config)#aaa server?% Unrecognized command occurs?

A. The router is a new device on which the aaa new-model command must be applied before continuing--

B. The command syntax requires a space after the word "server"

C. The command is invalid on the target device

D. The router is already running the latest operating system

78. What will be the potential consequence, if the native VLAN on a trunk is different on each end of the link?

A. The interface on both switches may shut down

B. The switch with the higher native VLAN may shut down

C. STP loops may occur

D. The interface with the lower native VLAN may shut down

79. When you apply an access list to a physical interface, which of the following option describes information that must be considered?

A. Direction of the access class

B. Direction of the access group --

C. Protocol used for filtering

D. Direction of the access list

80. Which one of the following source port does IKE use when NAT has been detected between two VPN gateways?

A. UDP 4500

B. TCP 4500

C. TCP 500

D. UDP 500

81. Which three of the following features are of IPsec transport mode? (Choose any three.)

A. IPsec transport mode supports unicast

B. IPsec transport mode encrypts only the payload

C. IPsec transport mode is used between end stations

D. IPsec transport mode is used between gateways

E. IPsec transport mode supports multicast

F. IPsec transport mode encrypts the entire packet

82. Which of the following command makes a Layer 2 switch interface to operate as a Layer 3 interface?

A. no switchport

B. no switchport nonnegotiate

C. switchport

D. no switchport mode dynamic auto

83. Which of the following security term refers to a person, property, or data of value to a company?

A. Risk

B. Asset

C. Threat prevention

D. Mitigation technique

84. Which of the following technology you can use to prevent non malicious program to run in the computer that is disconnected from the network?

A. Firewall

B. Software Antivirus

C. Network IP

D. Host IPS.

85. Which of the following command enable ospf authentication?

   A. ip ospf authentication message-digest

   B. network 192.168.10.0 0.0.0.255 area 0

   C. area 20 authentication message-digest

   D. ip ospf message-digest-key 1 md5 CCNA

86. Which of the following command help user1 to use enable, disable, exit commands?

   A. catalyst1(config)#username user1 privilege 1 secret us1pass

   B. catalyst1(config)#username user1 privilege 0 secret us1pass

   C. catalyst1(config)#username user1 privilege 5 secret us1pass

   D. catalyst1(config)#username user1 privilege 2 secret us1pass

87. Which of the following OSPF configuration command will not be required for MD5 authentication to work?

```
interface GigabitEthernet0/1
ip address 192.168.10.1 255.255.255.0
ip ospf authentication message-digest
ip ospf message-digest-key 1 md5 CCNA
!
router ospf 65000
router-id 192.168.10.1
area 20 authentication message-digest
network 10.1.1.0 0.0.0.255 area 10
network 192.168.10.0 0.0.0.255 area 0
!
```

   A. network 192.168.10.0 0.0.0.255 area 0

   B. ip ospf authentication message-digest

   C. area 20 authentication message-digest

   D. ip ospf message-digest-key 1 md5 CCNA

88. Which of the following two NAT types allows only objects or groups to reference

an IP address? (choose two)

A. dynamic PAT

B. static NAT

C. dynamic NAT

D. identity NAT

89. Which of the following port in a PVLAN can communicate with every other ports?

A. Promiscuous mode

B. Isolated mode

C. Community mode

D. None of the above

90. Which two of the following given commands result in a secure bootset? (Choose any two.)

A. secure boot-set

B. secure boot-files

C. secure boot-image

D. secure boot-config

91. What one of the following is an example of social engineering?

A. gaining access to server room by posing as IT

B. Watching other user put in username and password (something around there)

C. Gaining access to a building through an unlocked door.

D. Access to a computer using USB drive.

92. Which of the following prevent the company data from modification even when the data is in transit?

A. Confidentiality

B. Integrity

C. Availability

D. All of the above

93. Which one is an example of SYN flood attack?

    A. Man in the middle attack

    B. Denial of Service attack

    C. Spoofing attack

    D. Reconnaissance attack

94. Which of the following type of an IPS can identify worms that are propagating in a network?

    A. Anomaly-based IPS

    B. Reputation-based IPS

    C. Signature-based IPS

    D. None of the above

95. Which **of the** following command verifies phase 1 of an IPsec VPN on a Cisco router?

    A. show crypto map

    B. show crypto isakmp sa--

    C. show crypto ipsec sa

    D. show crypto engine connection active

96. Which of the following type of firewall can act on the behalf of the end device?

    A. Proxy

    B. Stateful packet

    C. Application

    D. Packet

97. Which of the following syslog severity level is level number 7?

    A. Warning

    B. Debugging

C. Informational

D. Notification

98. In which of the following threat, the victim tricked into entering username and password information at a disguised website?

A. Phishing--

B. Spoofing

C. Malware

D. Spam

99. Which of the following type of mirroring does SPAN technology perform?

A. Local mirroring over Layer 2

B. Remote mirroring over Layer 2

C. Remote mirroring over Layer 3

D. Local mirroring over Layer 3

100.   Which of the following network device does NTP authenticate?

A. Only the client device

B. The firewall and the client device

C. Only the time source

D. The client device and the time source

101. Which of the following Cisco product can help mitigate web-based attacks within a network?

A. Adaptive Security Appliance

B. Email Security Appliance

C. Web Security Appliance

D. Identity Services Engine

102.   Which of the following statement correctly describes the function of a private

VLAN?

A. A private VLAN partitions the Layer 3 broadcast domain of a VLAN into subdomains

B. A private VLAN partitions the Layer 2 broadcast domain of a VLAN into subdomains-

C. A private VLAN enables the creation of multiple VLANs using one broadcast domain

D. A private VLAN combines the Layer 2 broadcast domains of many VLANs into one major broadcast domain

103.   Which of the following hash type does Cisco use to validate the integrity of downloaded images?

A. Sha1

B. Md5

C. Sha2

D. Md1

104.   Which of the following Cisco feature can help us to mitigate spoofing attacks by verifying symmetry of the traffic path?

A. Unidirectional Link Detection

B. TrustSec

C. Unicast Reverse Path Forwarding-

D. IP Source Guard

105.   Which one the following is the most common Cisco Discovery Protocol version 1 attack?

A. MAC-address spoofing

B. Denial of Service

C. CAM-table overflow

D. VLAN hopping

106.   Which of the following is the Cisco preferred countermeasure to mitigate CAM

overflows?

A. Port security

B. IP source guard

C. Dynamic port security

D. Root guard

107. Which one of the following option is the most effective placement of an IPS device within the infrastructure?

A. Inline, before the internet router and firewall

B. Inline, behind the internet router and firewall

C. Promiscuously, after the Internet router and before the firewall

D. Promiscuously, before the Internet router and the firewall

108. Which of the following events will occur when the TACACS+ server returns an error, if a router configuration includes the line aaa authentication login default group tacacs+ enable? (Choose any two.)

A. The user will be prompted to authenticate using the enable password

B. Authentication attempts to the router will be denied

C. Authentication will use the router`s local database

D. Authentication attempts will be sent to the TACACS+ server

109. Which of the following alert protocol is used with Cisco IPS Manager Express to support up to 10 sensors?

A. SDEE

B. Syslog

C. SNMP

D. CSM

110. What is the first step that STP takes to prevent loops, when a switch has multiple links connected to a downstream switch?

A. STP selects the root port

B. STP elects the root bridge

C. STP selects the designated port

D. STP blocks one of the ports

111. Which of the following type of network address translation should be used when a Cisco ASA is in transparent mode?

A. Dynamic NAT

B. Static NAT

C. Overload

D. Dynamic PAT

112. Which of the following components does HMAC use to determine the authenticity and integrity of a message? (Choose any two.)

A. The password

B. The transform set

C. The hash

D. The key

113. What is the default timeout interval during which a router waits for responses from a TACACS server before declaring a timeout failure?

A. 10 seconds

B. 5 seconds

C. 15 seconds

D. 20 seconds

114. Which of the following countermeasures can mitigate ARP spoofing attacks? (Choose any two.)

A. DHCP snooping

B. IP source guard

C. Dynamic ARP inspection

D. Port security

115. Which of the following statements is true about access lists? (Choose any three.)
    A. Extended access lists should be placed as near as possible to the destination
    B. Extended access lists should be placed as near as possible to the source
    C. Standard access lists should be placed as near as possible to the destination
    D. Standard access lists filter on the source address
    E. Standard access lists filter on the destination address
    F. Standard access lists should be placed as near as possible to the source

116. Which of the following security measures can protect the control plane of a Cisco router? (Choose any two.)
    A. Parser views
    B. Access control lists
    C. Port security
    D. CCPr
    E. CoPP

117. In which of the following stage of an attack does the attacker discover devices on a target network?
    A. Covering tracks
    B. Reconnaissance
    C. Gaining access
    D. Maintaining access

118. Which of the following protocols use encryption to protect the confidentiality of data transmitted between two parties? (Choose any two.)
    A. SSH
    B. Telnet
    C. AAA
    D. FTP
    E. HTTPS

F. HTTP

119. What two of the following are the primary attack methods of VLAN hopping? (Choose any two.)

A. VoIP hopping

B. Double tagging

C. Switch spoofing

D. CAM-table overflow

120. Which two of the following are uses of SIEM software? (Choose any two.)

A. performing automatic network audits

B. collecting and archiving syslog data

C. alerting administrators to security events in real time

D. configuring firewall and IDS devices

E. scanning email for suspicious attachments

121. Which of the following are the three layers of a hierarchical network design? (Choose any three.)

A. user

B. access

C. core

D. distribution

E. server

F. Internet

122. In how many ways does the RADIUS protocol differ from TACACS? (Choose any three.)

A. RADIUS uses TCP to communicate with the NAS.

B. RADIUS can encrypt the entire packet that is sent to the NAS.

C. RADIUS supports per-command authorization.

D. RADIUS uses UDP to communicate with the NAS.

E. RADIUS encrypts only the password field in an authentication packet.

F. RADIUS authenticates and authorizes simultaneously, causing fewer packets to be transmitted.

G.

123. Which of the following three statements describe DHCP spoofing attacks? (Choose any three.)

A. They can access most network devices.

B. They protect the identity of the attacker by masking the DHCP address.

C. They can physically modify the network gateway.

D. They can modify traffic in transit.

E. They are used to perform man-in-the-middle attacks.

F. They use ARP poisoning.

124. Which of the following security principle will be violated if a data breach has occurred and your company database has been copied?

A. confidentiality

B. availability

C. access

D. control

125. In which of the following type of an attack does an attacker send email messages that ask the recipient to click a link such as https://www.cisco.net.cc/securelogon?

A. Pharming

B. Phishing

C. solicitation

D. secure transaction

126. Which of the following controls the user access to specific website category?

A. URL Filtering

B. URL Categorization

C. Spam filtering

D. Anti-malware protection (AMP)

127. What purpose does SSL/TLS decryption serve? (Choose any three)

A. It defines the rules and policies to allow or block specific application or data

B. It blocks hidden malware in encrypted SSL/TLS traffic

C. It detects and blocks Intrusion attempts from an attacker

D. It establishes SSL VPN

E. It provides data encryption and authentication

128. Which of the following is a web based attack?

A. cross site scripting (XSS)

B. SQL injection

C. file inclusion

D. cross site forgery

E. All of the above

F. None of the above

129. Which of the following statement provides the best definition of malware?

E. Malware is software used by nation states to commit cybercrimes.

F. Malware is unwanted software that is harmful or destructive.

G. Malware is a collection of worms, viruses, and Trojan horses that is distributed as a single package.

H. Malware is tools and applications that remove unwanted programs.

130. Which of the following mechanism does asymmetric cryptography use to secure data?

I. shared secret keys

J. a public/private key pair

K. an RSA nonce

L. an MD5 hash

131. Which of the following technique is the best way to confirm that AAA authentication is working properly?

    M. Ping the NAS to confirm connectivity.

    N. Use the Cisco-recommended configuration for AAA authentication.

    O. Use the test aaa command. ---

    P. Log into and out of the router, and then check the NAS authentication log

132. How EAP exchange is made secure by PEAP?

    A. It encrypts the exchange using the client certificate.

    B. It validates the server-supplied certificate, and then encrypts the exchange using the client certificate.

    C. It encrypts the exchange using the server certificate

    D. It validates the client-supplied certificate, and then encrypts the exchange using the server certificate.

133. How does EAP-FASTv2 is more efficient than EAP-FAST?

    A. It supports more secure encryption protocols.

    B. It allows multiple credentials to be passed in a single EAP exchange.

    C. It allows faster authentication by using fewer packets.

    D. It addresses security vulnerabilities found in the original protocol.

134. Which of the following configuration allows AnyConnect to automatically establish a VPN session when a user logs in to the computer?

    A. proxy

    B. transparent mode

    C. Trusted Network Detection

    D. always-on

135. Which of the following security feature allows a private IP address to access the Internet by translating it to a public address?

    A. hairpinning

B. NAT

C. Trusted Network Detection

D. Certification Authority

136. Refer to the following exhibit, given below:

R1
Interface GigabitEthernet 0/0
IP address 10.20.20.4 255.255.255.0

Crypto isakmp policy 1
Authentication pre-share
Lifetime 84600
Crypto isakmp key test7890 address 10.20.20.4

R2

Interface GigabitEthernet 0/0
IP address 10.20.20.4 255.255.255.0

Crypto isakmp policy 10
Authentication pre-share
Lifetime 84600
Crypto isakmp key test12345 address 10.30.30.5

You have configured R1 and R2 in the given context, but the routers are unable to establish a site-to-site VPN tunnel. Which of the following action can you take to correct the problem?

A. Edit the ISAKMP policy sequence numbers on R1 and R2 to match.

B. Set a valid value for the crypto key lifetime on each router.

C. Edit the crypto isakmp key command on each router with the address value of its own interface.

D. Edit the crypto keys on R1 and R2 to match.

137.   Refer to the following exhibit, given below:

> Crypto ipsec transform-set myset esp-md5-hmac esp-aes-256

How this command effects the configuration?

A. It merges authentication and encryption methods to protect traffic that matches an ACL.

B. It configures authentication as AES 256.

C. It configures the network to use a different transform set between peers.

D. It configures encryption for MD5 HMAC.

138.   Which of the following statement is true about IOS privilege levels?

A. Each privilege level supports the commands at its own level and all levels above it.

B. Each privilege level supports the commands at its own level and all levels below it.

C. Privilege-level commands are set explicitly for each user.

D. Each privilege level is independent of all other privilege levels.

139.   In the command "router ospf 200", what purpose does the value 200 serves?

A. administrative distance value

B. ABR ID

C. process ID

D. area ID

140.   Which of the following feature filters CoPP packets?

A. class maps

B. access control lists

C. policy maps

D. route maps

141. In which of the following type of an attack does the attacker dares to overload the CAM table on a switch so that the switch starts malfunctioning?

A. MAC spoofing

B. gratuitous ARP

C. DoS

D. MAC flooding

142. Which one of the following is a potential drawback of letting VLAN 1 as the native VLAN?

A. Gratuitous ARPs might be able to conduct a man-in-the-middle attack.

B. It may be susceptible to a VLAN hoping attack.

C. The CAM might be overloaded, effectively turning the switch into a hub.

D. VLAN 1 might be vulnerable to IP address spoofing.

143. Which of the following IPS mode provides the maximum number of actions?

A. failover

B. bypass

C. Inline

D. promiscuous

E. span

144. How false negative on an IPS can be detected?

A. Use a third-party system to perform penetration testing.

B. Use a third-party to audit the next-generation firewall rules.

C. View the alert on the IPS.

D. Review the IPS log.

E. Review the IPS console.

145. Which of the following is the primary purpose of a defined rule in an IPS?

A. to configure an event action that is pre-defined by the system administrator

B. to detect internal attacks

C. to configure an event action that takes place when a signature is triggered.

D. to define a set of actions that occur when a specific user logs in to the system

146.   Which of the following technology is used to rate data fidelity and to provide an authenticated hash for data?

A. signature updates

B. network blocking

C. file reputation

D. file analysis

147.   Which of the following is a benefit of a web application firewall?

A. It simplifies troubleshooting.

B. It accelerates web traffic.

C. It blocks known vulnerabilities without patching applications.

D. It supports all networking protocols.

148.   How FirePOWER block malicious email attachments?

A. It sends the traffic through a file policy.

B. It sends an alert to the administrator to verify suspicious email messages.

C. It forwards email requests to an external signature engine.

D. It scans inbound email messages for known bad URLs.

149.   Which of the following mechanism is applied, if a switch port goes directly into a blocked state only when a superior BPDU is received?

A. STP Root guard

B. EtherChannel guard

C. STP BPDU guard

D. loop guard

150.   Which of the following protocols must be allowed for an IPsec VPN tunnel

establishment and operation? (Choose any two.)

    A. 501

    B. 500

    C. 51

    D. 168

    E. 50

151. In which of the following terminology a sensor generates an alert about the traffic which is not malicious, but requires serious attention as long as security is concerned?

    A. true negative

    B. false positive

    C. false negative

    D. true positive

152. Which of the following is a part of digital signature and it determines the critical level of an attack?

    A. Attack Relevancy (AR)

    B. Global Correlation

    C. Attack Severity Rating (ASR)

    D. Signature Fidelity Rating (SFR)

153. Which of the following attack exploits the weakness of any software that are unknown by the software vendor?

    A. Man-in-the-middle attack

    B. Zero-day attack

    C. MAC overflow

    D. ARP Spoofing

    E. STP Attack

154. Which of the following is a limitation of an IPS?

    A. It introduces delay because every packet is analyzed before forwarded to

destination.

B. IPS does not responds immediately to an attack.

C. It works passively

D. None of the above.

155. Which of the following techniques does IPS provides for network protection by preventing an attack to reach its destination?

A. By enforcing policies

B. By controlling access to resources

C. By hardening networking devices

D. All of the above

E. None of the above

156. In which of the following configured mode the whole IP traffic will be dropped in case of sensor's failure?

A. 'fail-close' mode

B. 'fail-open' mode

C. Both of them

D. None of the above

157. Which of the following option helps you to create a blacklist, with the help of Cisco Collective Security Intelligence Team "Talos" (http://www.talosintel.com/)?

A. Static Blacklist

B. Dynamic Blacklist

C. Hybrid Blacklist

D. None of the above

158. The technique in which you allow or permit IP address or traffic of your own choice is referred to as:

A. Blacklisting

B. Whitelisting

C. Greylisting

D. None of the above

159. What of the following three key features of URL filtering? (Choose any three)

A. Predefined URL categories

B. Custom URL categories

C. Dynamic content analysis

D. Malware protection

160. Which one of the following is the most common type of spoofing? (choose any two)

A. Application spoofing

B. Service spoofing

C. DHCP spoofing

D. MAC address spoofing

E. Routing table spoofing

161. Which authentication mechanisms can be used with SNMP version 3? (Choose any two)

A. AES

B. 3DES

C. SHA

D. MD5

162. Which one of the following option is never part of an IKE Phase 2 process?

A. Specifying a hash (HMAC)

B. Running DH (PFS)

C. Main mode

D. Negotiating the transform set to use

163. Which of the following option mitigates VLAN Hopping and Double-tagging VLAN Hopping Attacks?

A. Ensuring that the native VLAN of the trunk ports is the same as the native VLAN of the user ports

B. Setting the trunk port to "off."

C. Enabling auto trunking negotiations.

D. Ensuring that the native VLAN of the trunk ports is different from the native VLAN of the user ports

164. Which of the following three statements about firewalls are true? (Choose any three)

A. A firewall can introduce a performance bottleneck.

B. If a system in a security zone is compromised, a firewall can help to contain the attack within that zone.

C. A firewall can prevent undesired access to a network security zone.

D. Modern firewalls provide a complete network security solution.

E. Firewalls typically provide protection between and within network security zones.

165. Which of the following type of an attack is prevented when you configure Secure Shell (SSH)?

A. DoS session spoofing

B. Man-in-the-middle attack

C. Dictionary attack

D. Buffer overflow

166. Which of the following type of traffic inspection uses pattern matching?

A. Signature–based inspection

B. Statistical anomaly detection

C. Protocol verification

D. Policy-based inspection

167. Which of the following type of VPN technology is likely to be used in a site-to-site VPN?

A. SSL

B. IPsec

C. TLS

D. HTTPS

168. What is a ping sweep?

   A. A scanning technique that indicates the range of TCP or UDP port numbers on a host.

   B. A network scanning technique that indicates the number of live hosts in a range of IP addresses.

   C. A solution that provides data security through encryption.

   D. A query and response protocol that identifies information about a domain, including the addresses that are assigned to that domain.

169. Which three are the main components of information security? (Choose any three)

   A. Threat prevention

   B. Authorization

   C. Confidentiality

   D. Countermeasures

   E. Integrity

   F. Availability

170. Which three characteristics describe SIEM technology? (Choose any three)

   A. It provides a comprehensive and centralized view of an IT infrastructure.

   B. It establishes VPN connection.

   C. It provides real-time analysis of logs and security alerts generated by network hardware or application.

   D. It saves data for the long time, so the organizations can have a detailed report of incident.

   E. It prevents man-in-the-middle attack.

171. Databases that categorizes the threats over the internet are known as:

   A. Common Vulnerabilities and Exposures (CVE)

   B. Simple Network Monitoring Protocol (SNMP)

C. Simple Mail Transfer Protocol (SMTP)

D. Intrusion Prevention System (IPS)

172. Which of the followings is an availability attack?

A. Denial of service (DOS) attack

B. DHCP snooping

C. Botnet

D. Phishing

E. Port security

173. Which of the followings are the attack generating methods? (Choose any three)

A. Social Engineering

B. Port security

C. Reconnaissance

D. Pharming

E. DHCP Snooping

174. Which attack denies services reduce the functionality or prevent the access of the resources even to the legitimate users?

A. Denial-of-Service (DoS) attack

B. DHCP spoofing

C. Botnet

D. Phishing

E. Pharming

175. Which of the two network security solutions can be used to prevent DoS attacks? (Choose any two)

A. Virus Scanning

B. Intrusion Protection Systems (IPS)

C. Applying User Authentication

D. Anti-Spoofing Technologies

E. Data Encryption

176. An attacker with a laptop (rogue access point) is capturing all network traffic from a targeted user. Which type of attack is this?

A. DHCP spoofing

B. MAC overflow

C. Man-in-the-Middle

D. Whaling

177. What is the characteristic of a Trojan horse?

A. A Trojan is a self-replicating malware, which infects system, files or programs.

B. A Trojan horse carries out malicious operations under the guise of a legitimate program.

C. Malicious software, which is designed to disguise itself misleading users of its true intent.

D. A malicious software application, which delivers ads through pop-up windows on any program's interface.

178. What is the characteristic of a worm malware?

A. A worm must be triggered by an event on the host system.

B. A malicious software application, which delivers ads through pop-up windows on any program's interface.

C. Once installed on a host system, a worm does not replicate itself.

D. A worm is a self-replicating malware, which infects system, files or programs.

179. An attacker is using Wireshark to discover administrative Telnet usernames and passwords. What type of network attack does this describe?

A. Denial of Service

B. Reconnaissance

C. Port Redirection

D. Trust Exploitation

180. Which malicious software is designed to encrypt user's data and then hackers demand ransom payment to decrypt the respective data?

A. Ransomware

B. Scareware

C. Worms

D. Adware

181. Which attack involves a software program attempting to discover a system password by using an electronic dictionary?

A. Denial of Service attack

B. Brute-Force attack

C. IP Spoofing attack

D. Man-in-the-Middle attack

E. Port Redirection attack

182. Which type of network has the topology where multiple LANs are interconnected but it is not expanded as Wide Area Network (WAN) or Metropolitan Area Network (MAN)?

A. Campus Area Network

B. Cloud and Wide Area Network

C. Data Center

D. Small Office/Home Office (SOHO)

183. The technique of encrypting the clear text data into a scrambled code is called:

A. AAA authentication

B. Cryptography

C. Cisco Discovery protocol (CDP)

D. Cypher text

184. Which type of cryptography uses the same pair of keys on both sides?
    A. Asymmetric Key Cryptography
    B. Public Key Cryptography
    C. Symmetric Key Cryptography
    D. Hybrid Key Cryptography

185. The combination of policies, procedures, hardware, software, and people that are required to create, manage and revoke digital certificates is called?
    A. Service Level Agreement (SLA)
    B. Certificate Authority (CA)
    C. Public Key Infrastructure (PKI)
    D. None of the above

186. Which kind of potential threat can occur by Instant On in a data center?
    A. When the primary firewall in the data center crashes.
    B. When an attacker hijacks a VM hypervisor and then launches attacks against other devices in the data center.
    C. When the primary IPS appliance is malfunctioning.
    D. When a VM that may have outdated security policies is brought online after a long period of inactivity.

187. What role does the Security Intelligence Operations (SIO) play in Network architecture?
    A. User authentication
    B. Policy enforcement
    C. Resource management
    D. Identify and stop malicious traffic

188. What is the primary method of network defense for mitigating malware?
    A. Make use of encrypted or hashed authentication protocols.
    B. Install antivirus scanner or software on all hosts.

C. Deploy intrusion prevention systems on the entire network.

D. Deploy firewalls.

189. What usually motivates cyber attackers or criminals to attack networks as compared to hacktivists or state-sponsored hackers?

A. Political reasons

B. Fame seeking

C. Network vulnerability testing

D. Financial gain

190. What purpose does a digital certificate serve?

A. It makes sure that a website has not been hacked.

B. It authenticates a website and establishes a secure connection to exchange confidential data.

C. It provides proof that data has a traditional signature attached.

D. It ensures that the person who is gaining access to a network device is authorized.

191. Which of the following is a type of encryption algorithm that uses a pair of public and private keys to provide authentication, integrity, and confidentiality?

A. Symmetric

B. Shared Secret

C. Both A and D

D. Asymmetric

192. Which of the following type of an encryption algorithm uses the same key to encrypt and decrypt data?

A. RSA

B. Shared-Secret

C. Public-Key

D. Asymmetric

193. What is the main feature of Control Plane Policing (CoPP)?
    A. Reduce overall traffic by disabling control plane services.
    B. Configuration, management and monitoring of networking devices.
    C. Manage services provided by the control plane.
    D. Restrict unnecessary traffic from overloading the route processor.

194. What are the types of role-based CLI control access feature?
    A. Super view, admin view, config view, CLI view
    B. admin view, Root view, CLI view, Super view
    C. root view, CLI view, Super view, admin view
    D. CLI view, Root view, Super view, Law intercept view

195. By default, what is the privilege level of user account created on Cisco routers?
    A. 0
    B. 1
    C. 15
    D. 16

196. Syslog server uses eight severity levels from zero, which of the following level indicates the critical condition?
    A. 0
    B. 1
    C. 2
    D. 3
    E. 4
    F. None

197. An application-level network monitoring protocol with fewer manager stations and controls a set of agents, known as:
    A. HTML

B. TCP

C. SNMP

D. SMTP

198. Which one is the characteristic of the MIB?

A. OIDs are organized in a hierarchical structure.

B. Information in the MIB is rigid.

C. A separate MIB tree exists for any given device in the network.

D. Information is organized in a flat manner so that SNMP can access it quickly.

199. _____ is the process of proving an identity of a user by login identification and a password.

A. Authorization

B. Authentication

C. Accounting

D. MIB

200. Which AAA security protocol provides encryption of full payload?

A. RADIUS

B. TACACS

C. ISE

D. ACS

201. What is the requirement to enable the Secure Copy Protocol feature in a network?

A. A user with privilege level 1 has to be configured for local authentication.

B. SSH protocol has to be configured and a command must be issued to enable the SCP server side functionality.

C. Transfer can only occur from SCP clients that are routers.

D. Telnet protocol has to be configured first on the SCP server side.

202. Which specification or protocol provides port based network access control (PNAC)?

    A. 802.1Q

    B. 802.1

    C. 802.1x

    D. None of the above

203. Which technology provides seamless connectivity between network and end users while maintaining good security policies for an organization?

    A. IOT

    B. BYOD

    C. SNMP

    D. FTP

204. Which solution provides the unified management of the entire network (mobile devices, smart phones, tablets, notebooks, Laptops etc.) from a centralized dashboard?

    A. BYOD

    B. IOT

    C. MDM

    D. Big Data

205. Which option can be configured by Cisco AutoSecure?

    A. Enable secret password

    B. Interface IP address

    C. SNMP

    D. Syslog

206. After enabling AAA, which three CLI steps are required to configure a router with a parser view? (Choose any three)

    A. Create a root view using the parser view view-name command.

B. Associate the view with the law intercept view.

C. Assign groups who can use the view.

D. Create a view using the parser view view-name command.

E. Assign a secret password to the view.

F. Assign commands to the view.

207. In SSH, which three steps are required to configure Router to accept only encrypted SSH connections? (Choose any three)

A. Enable inbound vty SSH sessions.

B. Assign IP addresses.

C. Configure DNS on the router.

D. Configure IP domain name on the router.

E. Enable Telnet sessions.

F. Generate SSH keys.

208. What are the three primary functions of syslog logging service? (Choose any three)

A. Specifies the size of the logging buffer.

B. Specifies the database where captured information is stored.

C. Gathers logging information.

D. Compares the information to be captured and the information to be ignored.

E. Authenticates and encrypts data sent revolving inside LAN.

F. Assigns time stamp to the packets.

209. On which plane or layer do we apply policies to control user traffic?

A. Data plane

B. Control plane

C. Management plane

D. None of the above

210. Which plane involves the configuration, management and monitoring of

networking devices?

A. Data plane

B. Control plane

C. Management plane

D. None of the above

211. Which of the following version of SNMP supports encryption and hashing?

A. Version 1

B. Version 2c

C. Version 3

D. All

212. Which protocol allows networking devices to synchronize their time with respect to the NTP server, so the devices may have more authenticated time settings and generated syslog messages?

A. Syslog

B. NTP

C. SNMP

D. SMTP

213. What functional plane is responsible for device-generated packets required for network operation, such as ARP message exchanges and routing advertisements?

A. Data plane

B. Control plane

C. Management plane

D. Forwarding plane

214. If a user complains about not being able to gain access to a network device configured with AAA. How would the network administrator determine if login access for the user account is disabled or not?

A. Use the show aaa user command.

B. Use the show aaa local user lockout command.

C. Use the show running-configuration command.

D. Use the show aaa sessions command.

215. Which AAA solution supports both RADIUS and TACACS+ servers?

A. RADIUS and TACACS+ servers cannot be supported by a single solution.

B. Implement a local database.

C. Implement Cisco Secure Access Control System (ACS) only.

D. Access Control System (ACS).

216. Syslog server uses eight severity levels from zero, which of the following level indicates the WARNING condition?

A. 0

B. 1

C. 2

D. 3

E. 4

F. None

217. Which of the following logging mechanism provides time stamp of an event?

A. SCP

B. NTP

C. Syslog logging

D. SNMP

218. Which statement best describes a VPN connection?

A. VPNs use virtual connections to create a secure tunnel over a public network.

B. VPNs use dedicated physical connections to transfer data between connected users.

C. VPNs use logical connections to create public networks over the Internet.

D. VPNs use open source virtualization software to create the tunnel through the

Internet.

219. Which are the key features of VPN technology? (Choose any four)
   A. Confidentiality
   B. Virtualization
   C. Data integrity
   D. Authentication
   E. Anti-replay Protection
   F. Authorization

220. Which of the following VPN offers end-user connectivity?
   A. Site-to-site VPN
   B. Remote access VPN
   C. Hybrid VPN
   D. None

221. Which of the following VPN technologies are used today? (Choose any three)
   A. IPsec
   B. SSL
   C. HTTPS
   D. MPLS
   E. SMTP

222. Which of the protocol provides confidentiality integrity, and authentication services and is a type of VPN?
   A. ESP
   B. IPsec
   C. MD5
   D. AES

223. What three protocols must be permitted for the establishment of IPsec site-to-

site VPNs? (Choose any three)

A. SSH

B. AH

C. ISAKMP

D. NTP

E. ESP

F. HTTPS

224. During the establishment of an IPsec VPN tunnel, when is the security association (SA) created?

A. During Phase 1

B. During Phase 2

C. During both Phase 1 and 2

D. None of the above

225. Which action takes place during the IKE Phase 2 exchange of IPsec peer establishment?

A. Negotiation of IKE policy sets

B. Exchange of keep alive packets

C. Negotiation of IPsec policy

D. Exchange of Hello packets

226. Which of the following statements describe the IPsec protocol framework? (Choose any two)

A. AH provides integrity and authentication.

B. ESP provides encryption, authentication, and integrity.

C. AH uses IP protocol 40.

D. AH provides encryption and integrity.

227. Which of the two IPsec protocols are used to provide data integrity?

A. AES

B. DH

C. MD5

D. RSA

E. SHA

228. Which of the following protocols must be allowed for an IPsec VPN tunnel establishment and operation? (Choose any two)

A. 501

B. 500

C. 51

D. 168

E. 50

229. Which one is the characteristic of remote-access VPNs?

A. The VPN configuration is identical between the remote devices.

B. The VPN connection is initiated by the remote user.

C. Internal hosts have no knowledge of the VPN.

D. Information required to establish the VPN must remain static.

230. Which mode of IPsec encapsulate only payload field while the original IP headers remain unchanged?

A. Tunnel mode

B. Transport mode

C. Both tunnel and transport mode

D. None of the above

231. Which of the VPN is provided by the internet service provider to allow an organization with two or more branches to have logical connectivity between the sites using the service provider's network for transport?

A. SSL

B. IPSec

C. MPLS

D. None of the above

232. What purpose does NAT-Traversal feature serves?

A. Disables NAT for VPN clients

B. Allows NAT to work transparently on one or both ends of the VPN connection

C. Makes NAT to be used for IPv6 addresses

D. Upgrades NAT for IPv4

233. The situation where VPN traffic that is received by an interface is routed back out that same interface is known as _____.

A. GRE

B. MPLS

C. Hair-pinning

D. Split-tunnelling

234. Refer to the exhibit. Which algorithm is used here for providing confidentiality?

```
R1(config)# crypto isakmp policy 1

R1(config-isakmp)# hash md5

R1(config-isakmp)# encryption des

R1(config-isakmp)#group 2

R1(config-isakmp)#lifetime 3600

R1(config-isakmp)#authentication pre-share
```

A. RSA

B. Diffie-Hellman

C. DES

D. AES

235.   Which is the best transform amongst all to provide protection?

   A. crypto ipsec transform-set ESP-DES-SHA esp-3des esp-sha-hmac

   B. crypto ipsec transform-set ESP-DES-SHA esp-des esp-sha-hmac

   C. crypto ipsec transform-set ESP-DES-SHA esp-aes esp-des esp-sha-hmac

   D. crypto ipsec transform-set ESP-DES-SHA esp-aes-256 esp-sha-hmac

236.   What is the main function of the Diffie-Hellman algorithm inside the IPsec framework?

   A. Provides encryption

   B. Provides authentication

   C. Allows peers to exchange shared keys

   D. Guarantees message delivery

237.   Refer to the exhibit. Which algorithm is used here for providing data integrity?

   R1(config)# crypto isakmp policy 1

   R1(config-isakmp)# hash md5

   R1(config-isakmp)# encryption des

   R1(config-isakmp)#group 2

   R1(config-isakmp)#lifetime 3600

   R1(config-isakmp)#authentication pre-share

   A. SHA

   B. MD5

   C. DES

   D. AES

238.   In order to implement security on all company routers, which two commands must be issued to implement authentication via the password "IPSpecialist" for all OSPF-enabled interfaces in the backbone area of the company network? (Choose any two)

   A. area 1 authentication message-digest

B. area 0 authentication message-digest

C. ip ospf message-digest-key 1 md5 IPSpecialist

D. username OSPF password IPSpecialist

E. enable password IPSpecialist

239. What purpose does the command "ip ospf message-digest-key key md5 password" serve?

A. To configure OSPF MD5 authentication globally on the router

B. To enable OSPF MD5 authentication on a per-interface basis

C. To facilitate the establishment of neighbor adjacencies

D. To enable OSPF MD5 authentication on a per-port basis

240. Which of the followings is the characteristic of the Cisco IOS Resilient Configuration feature?

A. It creates a secure working copy of the bootstrap startup program.

B. Once issued, the secure boot-config command automatically upgrades the configuration archive to a newer version.

C. A snapshot of running configuration of the router can be taken and securely archived in a storage device.

D. The secure boot-image command works properly when the system is configured to run an image from a TFTP server.

241. What purpose does the show "ip ospf neighbour" command serve?

A. Shows the list of active interfaces

B. Shows the list OSPF neighbors

C. Shows the list best routes

D. All of the above

242. Which type of switching cache makes the route for the session in advance even before any packets need to be processed?

A. Process switching

B. Fast switching

C. Cisco Express Forwarding (CEF)

D. None of the above

243. What are the two main components of Cisco Express Forwarding (CEF) that are needed to perform its function? (Choose any two)

A. Forwarding Information Base (FIB)

B. Routing table

C. Adjacency table

D. MAC table

244. What is the main function of Control Plane Policing (CoPP) feature?

A. Disable all control plane services to reduce overall traffic

B. Direct all excess traffic to the route processor

C. Manage services provided by the data plane

D. Restricts unnecessary traffic from overloading the route processor

245. Which of the following are common layer 2 attacks?

A. STP attack

B. MAC Spoofing

C. MAC table overflow

D. VLAN hopping

E. ALL

246. A type of an attack in which an attacker actively listens for ARP broadcasts and sends its own MAC address for given IP address is known as _____.

A. STP attack

B. ARP Spoofing

C. MAC table overflow

D. VLAN hopping

247. A technique of manipulating MAC address to impersonate the legitimate user

or launch an attack such as Denial-of-Service attack is known as _____.

A. STP attack

B. MAC Spoofing

C. MAC table overflow

D. VLAN hopping

248. Which of the following methods serve as the mitigation technique for DHCP spoofing?

A. Port security

B. Dynamic ARP inspection

C. DHCP Snooping

D. Cisco discovery protocol (CDP)

249. Which of the followings is the mitigation technique of layer 2 attacks?

A. Port security

B. Dynamic ARP inspection

C. DHCP Snooping

D. All of the above

E. None

250. Which feature of STP prevents loop creation after STP is converged and redundant links are disabled?

A. BPDU guard

B. Loop guard

C. Root guard

D. None of the above

251. Which of the followings is the characteristic of port security?

A. It binds the MAC address of known devices to the physical port and associates it with violation action

B. It determines the best route for routing

C. It provides authentication and encryption

D. None of the above

252. What purpose does the "show ip dhcp snooping binding" command serve?

A. Shows the list of active interfaces

B. Shows the list OSPF neighbors

C. Shows the list best routes

D. Shows clients list with the legitimate IP addresses assigned to them

253. In which type of an attack does an attacker sends bogus requests for broadcasting to DHCP server with spoofed MAC addresses to lease all IP addresses in DHCP address pool?

A. STP attack

B. MAC Spoofing

C. MAC table overflow

D. DHCP Starvation

254. How can you prevent a VLAN hopping attack? (Choose any three)

A. Disable auto-trunking and enable manual-trunking

B. Enable auto-trunking

C. Change the native VLAN to a VLAN other than VLAN1

D. Always consider VLAN 1 as native VLAN

E. Tag the native VLAN traffic in order to prevent against 802.1Q double-tagging attack to exploit network vulnerability

255. What causes can lead to buffer overflow?

A. Overloading a system by downloading and installing too many software updates on a system at one time

B. If there is an attempt to write more data to a memory location than that location can hold

C. Overloading too much information to two or more interfaces of the same device, leading to packet dropping

D. All of the above

256. Which type of VLAN-hopping attack may be prevented by configuring any other VLAN as the native VLAN rather than VLAN 1?

A. DTP spoofing

B. DHCP spoofing

C. VLAN double-tagging

D. DHCP starvation

257. In order to mitigate VLAN hopping attacks, which of the following protocol should be disabled?

A. STP

B. DTP

C. ARP

D. CDP

258. On which type of port, can isolated port forward traffic to on a private VLAN?

A. On a community port

B. On a promiscuous port

C. On an isolated port

D. None of the above

259. What security measures prevent CAM table overflow attacks?

A. DHCP snooping

B. Dynamic ARP Inspection

C. IP source guard

D. Port security

260. In spanning Tree Protocol (STP), what security benefit is gained from enabling BPDU guard on Portfast enabled interfaces?

A. It prevents rogue switches from being part of a network

B. Assigns root bridges

C. It prevents buffer overflow attacks

D. Prevents Layer 2 loops

261.   Which of the following VPN solutions allows the establishment of a secure remote-access VPN tunnel between a web browser and the ASA?

A. clientless SSL

B. clientless IPSec

C. client-based SSL

D. client-based IPSec

262.   Which of the following protocols supports secure access provided by Cisco AnyConnect?

A. SSL only

B. IPsec only

C. SNMP

D. Both SSL and IPsec

E. None of the above

263.   Which of the following security features are provided by firewall? (Choose any three)

A. It does not provide user authentication.

B. It has the ability to inspect the traffic of more than just IP and port level.

C. By integrating with AAA, firewall can permit or deny traffic based on AAA policy.

D. By integrating with IPS/ID, firewall can detect and filter malicious data at the edge of network to protect the end-users.

E. It does not support encryption and authentication.

264.   Which of the firewalls provides granular control over the traffic by using information up to layer 7 of OSI model?

A. Circuit-Level Firewall

B. Application-Level Firewall

C. Stateful firewall

D. Next generation firewall

265. Which of the following firewalls operates at the session layer of the OSI model?

A. Circuit-Level Firewall

B. Application-Level Firewall

C. Stateful firewall

D. Next generation firewall

266. What is the advantage of using a Stateful firewall instead of a proxy server?

A. It performs user authentication.

B. It provides packet filtering.

C. It prevents Layer 7 attacks.

D. It provides better performance.

267. Which of the followings is the limitation of a Stateful firewall?

A. It is not as effective with UDP- or ICMP-based traffic.

B. It does not provide user authentication.

C. It does not filter unnecessary traffic.

D. It provides poor log information.

268. Which of the following steps must be taken after zones have been created in a Cisco IOS Zone-based firewall?

A. Assign interfaces to zones.

B. Apply encryption and authentication to the zones.

C. Disable the zones.

D. Establish policies between zones.

269. Which of the following firewalls monitors network traffic and determines

whether the packets belong to an existing connection or are from an unauthorized source?

A. Stateless firewall

B. Personal firewall

C. Application proxy

D. Stateful firewall

270. Which one of the following commands verifies a Zone-Based Policy Firewall configuration?

A. show interfaces

B. show zones

C. show running-config

D. show protocols

271. Which one of the followings is the function of state or session table?

A. It saves the best route information for routing.

B. It saves MAC addresses.

C. It saves NATing information.

D. It saves the state of current sessions in a table.

272. The global address either router's interface IP or one from pool, which will represent the client over an internet is termed as _____.

A. Inside Local

B. Inside Global

C. Outside Local

D. Outside Global

273. Which class of Cisco Common Classification Policy Language (C3PL) filters out the traffic that needs to be inspected?

A. Policy map

B. Class map

C. Service policies

D. None

274. Which class of Cisco Common Classification Policy Language (C3PL) inspects (Stateful inspection of traffic), permit (permit the traffic but no Stateful inspection), drop the traffic or generate log of it?

A. Policy map

B. Class map

C. Service policies

D. None

275. Which of the following two actions can be applied to a traffic class when a Cisco IOS Zone-Based Policy Firewall is being configured? (Choose any three)

A. Drop

B. Permit

C. Forward

D. Hold

E. Inspect

F. Copy

276. Which of the followings are the techniques of accessing firewall for management? (Choose any three)

A. OPManager

B. Command Line Interface (CLI)

C. ASA Security Device Manager (ASDMo)

D. Cisco security manager (CSM)

E. Simple network management protocol (SNMP)

F. None of the above

277. Which of the following actions in a Cisco IOS Zone-Based Policy Firewall is similar to a permit statement in an ACL?

A. Drop

B. Pass

C. Forward

D. Hold

E. Inspect

F. Copy

278. In a Cisco IOS Zone-Based Policy Firewall, what is the main function of the permit or pass action?

A. Drops suspected packets.

B. Forwards traffic from one zone to another.

C. Performs inspection of traffic between zones for traffic control.

D. Tracks the state of connections between zones.

279. In which mode of firewall deployment does ASA work as layer 2 bridge and traffic flows through it without adding itself as routing hop between communicating peers?

A. Routed mode

B. Transparent mode

C. Tunnel mode

D. Transport mode

E. None of the above

280. Which two of the followings are the modes of ASA deployment?

A. Routed mode

B. Transparent mode

C. Both Routed and Transparent mode

D. Transport mode

E. None of the above

281. In which method of High availability does one device act as primary firewall or

active firewall while the second stay in standby mode?

A. Active/Standby failover

B. Active/Active failover

C. Both of the above

D. None of the above

282. The concept of implementing multiple virtual firewalls is known as
_____.

A. Context

B. High availability

C. Security level

D. None of the above

283. Security level 100- is the highest possible and most trusted level. By default, on which of the following interface it is used?

A. On inside interface

B. On outside interface

C. On DMZ interface

D. None of the above

284. Which policy specifies the rules for the data traffic inbound or outbound passing through an interface?

A. Security Access policy

B. Firewall Management Policy

C. Network Connection Policy

D. All of the above

285. Which of the following algorithm can ensure data confidentiality?

A. AES

B. MD5

C. PKI

D. RSA

286. Why is asymmetric algorithm key management simpler than symmetric algorithm key management?

   A. Two public keys are used for the key exchange.

   B. It uses fewer bits.

   C. Only one key is used.

   D. One of the keys can be made public.

287. Data Encryption Standard (DES) uses _____ bits for data encryption.

   A. 42 bits

   B. 56 bits

   C. 61 bits

   D. 78 bits

288. Which of the following attacks exploits the weakness of any software that are unknown to the software vendor/developer?

   A. Man-in-the-Middle Attack

   B. Zero-Day Attack

   C. MAC Overflow

   D. ARP Spoofing

   E. STP Attack

289. What are the two common characteristics of the IDS and the IPS? (Choose any two)

   A. Both analyze copies of network traffic.

   B. Both mitigate the network attacks either actively or passively.

   C. Both are deployed as sensors.

   D. Both use signatures to detect malicious traffic.

   E. Both of them are placed in line with the network

290. Which of the followings are two limitations of an IDS? (Choose any two)

A. The IDS analyzes actual forwarded packets.

B. The IDS has great impact on traffic.

C. The IDS works offline using copies of network traffic.

D. The IDS requires other devices to respond to attacks.

E. The IDS does not stop malicious traffic.

291.   Where can an IDS/IPS be placed?

A. In Inside Zone

B. In Outside Zone

C. In DMZ Zone

D. All of the above

292.   Which of the followings is the limitation of network-based IPS as compared to host-based IPS?

A. Network-based IPS is less cost-effective.

B. Network-based IPS should not be used with multiple operating systems.

C. Network-based IPS does not detect lower level network events.

D. Network-based IPS cannot analyze encrypted traffic.

293.   In which of the following terminologies is a sensor that generates an alert about the traffic, which is not malicious, but requires serious attention as long as security is concerned?

A. True Negative

B. False Positive

C. False Negative

D. True Positive

294.   In which of the following terminologies is a malicious activity that is detected by the IPS module or sensor and for which an alert will be generated?

A. True Negative

B. False Positive

C. False Negative

D. True Positive

295. Which of the followings is a tool or technique for malicious traffic detection?
    A. Signature based IDS/IPS
    B. Policy based IDS/IPS
    C. Anomaly based IDS/IPS
    D. All of the above

296. Which one of the followings is the characteristic of Reputation Based IDS/IPS?
    A. To detect lower level network events.
    B. To collect the information from the systems participating in global correlation and filter out sites or URLs with bad reputation.
    C. To define security policies on the networking devices.
    D. To analyze specific string or behavior in a single packet or stream of packets to detect the anomaly.

297. Which of the following actions or responses are commonly used in IDS technology? (Choose any two)
    A. Drop
    B. Alert
    C. Reset
    D. Monitor
    E. Block

298. Which of the following actions define actions or responses that are commonly used in IPS technology?
    A. Drop
    B. Reset
    C. Block
    D. Shun
    E. All of the above

299. Which of the following micro-engines designs a signature to analyze a single

packet instead of stream of packets?

A. Atomic

B. Service

C. String or multistring

D. None of the above

300. Which of the followings is a part of digital signature and determines the critical level of an attack?

A. Attack Relevancy (AR)

B. Global Correlation

C. Attack Severity Rating (ASR)

D. Signature Fidelity Rating (SFR)

301. What is a disadvantage of a pattern-based detection mechanism?

A. The normal network traffic pattern will be disturbed.

B. It cannot detect unknown attacks.

C. It is not scalable.

D. Its configuration is complex.

302. Which of the following features of an IPS provides regular threat updates from the Cisco Network database?

A. Simple Network Monitoring Protocol (SNMP)

B. Event Correlation

C. Global Correlation

D. IPS Manager Express

303. In which mode of deployment will a copy of every data packet be sent to the sensor to analyze if there is any malicious activity?

A. Promiscuous or passive mode

B. Inline mode

C. Tap mode

D. None of the above

304. In which of the following configured modes will the whole IP traffic be dropped, in case of sensor failure?
   A. 'fail-close' mode
   B. 'fail-open' mode
   C. Both of them
   D. None of the above

305. Which of the following options helps you to create a blacklist, with the help of Cisco Collective Security Intelligence Team "Talos"?
   A. Static Blacklist
   B. Dynamic Blacklist
   C. Hybrid Blacklist
   D. None of the above

306. The technique in which you allow or permit IP address or traffic of your own choice is referred to as _____.
   A. Blacklisting
   B. Whitelisting
   C. Greylisting
   D. None of the above

307. Which of the followings is a limitation of an IPS?
   A. It introduces delay because every packet is analyzed before forwarded to destination.
   B. IPS does not respond immediately to an attack.
   C. It works passively.
   D. None of the above.

308. Which of the following techniques does IPS provide for network protection by

preventing an attack to reach its destination?

A. By enforcing policies.

B. By controlling access to resources.

C. By hardening networking devices.

D. All of the above.

E. None of the above.

309. Which of the followings are E-mail based threats?

A. Phishing attack

B. Spam

C. Malware attachment

D. All of the above

E. None of the above

310. Which of the following attacks tries to get login credentials by manipulating the end-user by presenting different links, which look legitimate?

A. Phishing attack

B. Spam

C. Malware attachment

D. Ransomware attack

311. Which of the followings are the features of Cisco's E-mail Security Appliance (ESA)? (Choose any three)

A. Network Monitoring

B. E-mail Encryption

C. Network Anti-virus

D. Physical Layer Security

E. Access Control

F. Easy VPN Access

312. Which of the followings is a feature of Anti-malware Protection Security Solution?

A. File retrospection

B. File sandboxing

C. File reputation

D. All of the above

E. None of the above

313. Which of the following features of Anti-malware protection analyzes file's behavior to determine the threat level and then updates the treat and its mitigations globally?

A. File retrospection

B. File sandboxing

C. File reputation

D. All of the above

E. None of the above

314. Which of the followings is a type of spam filtering that identifies spam messages without blocking the legitimate E-mail?

A. Reputation-Based Filtering

B. Context-Based Filtering

C. Both of the above

D. None of them

315. Which of the followings provides continuous analysis of data to detect, analyze, track, confirm and mitigate threats before, during and after an attack?

A. Spam Filtering

B. Data Loss Prevention (DLP)

C. Anti-Malware Protection(AMP)

D. E-mail Encryption

E. None of the above

316. Which of the followings is a characteristic of the Data Loss Prevention (DLP)?

A. Establishes VPN

B. Deep content analysis

C. E-mail integration

D. Spam Filtering

317.   Which of the followings is the most widely used E-mail encryption standard?
   A. Pretty Good Privacy (PGP)
   B. GNU Privacy Guard (GnuPG)
   C. Web-based E-mail encryption services
   D. None of the above

318.   Which of the followings controls the user access to specific website category?
   A. URL Filtering
   B. URL Categorization
   C. Spam Filtering
   D. Anti-Malware Protection (AMP)

319.   Which of the followings protects your web or mobile applications from being compromised and prevents data from breaching?
   A. Malware Scanning
   B. Spam Filtering
   C. Web Application Filtering
   D. Anti-Malware Protection (AMP)

320.   What purposes does SSL/TLS decryption serve? (Choose any three)
   A. It defines the rules and policies to allow or block specific application or data.
   B. It blocks hidden malware in encrypted SSL/TLS traffic.
   C. It detects and blocks intrusion attempts from an attacker.
   D. It establishes SSL VPN.
   E. It provides data encryption and authentication.

321.   Which of the followings are the mitigation techniques of Web based threats? (Choose any three)
   A. Web Application Firewall (WAF)
   B. Cloud Based Web Security (CWS)
   C. Cisco Web Security Appliance(WSA)
   D. E-mail Security Appliance (ESA)
   E. Native VLAN

F. Private VLAN

322. Which of the following ASA series is suitable for small to medium sized enterprise environment?

A. Cisco C170
B. Cisco C370
C. Cisco C380
D. Cisco C680

323. Which of the followings is a web based attack?

A. Cross-site scripting (XSS)
B. SQL injection
C. File inclusion
D. Cross-site forgery
E. All of the above
F. None of the above

324. Which of the following data state encryptions is provided by the software like TrueCrypt, AxCrypt BitLocker, MAC OS X FileVault?

A. Data in motion
B. Data at rest
C. VPN data
D. E-mail data

325. Which of the followings are the different protocols, which can be used in VPN implementation? (Choose any three)

A. Generic Routing Encapsulation (GRE)
B. Multiprotocol Label Switching (MPLS) VPN
C. Internet Protocol Security (IPsec)
D. TCP
E. UDP

326. Host based intrusion prevention system (HIPS) is replaced by?

A. Advanced Malware Protection (AMP)

B. URL Filtering

C. URL Categorization

D. None of the above

Answers

1. **C, E** (AES, SHA-384)

Explanation: Cisco NGE technology offers a complete algorithm by using

- Elliptic curve cryptography (ECC) to replace RSA and DH
- Galois/Counter Mode (GCM) of the Advanced Encryption Standard (AES) block cipher for high-speed authenticated encryption
- SHA-2 for Hashing operations to replace MD5 and SHA-1

2. **B, C, D** (DNS, BOOTP, TFTP)

Explanation: The ACL default is configured on the port of access layer switch to prevent un-authorized access. ACL-DEFAULT only allows DNS, DHCP, ICMP, and TFTP traffic and denies everything else.

3. **A, B, C** (Software as a Service, Infrastructure as a Service, Platform as a Service)

Explanation: The three main types of cloud computing service model: SaaS, PaaS, and IaaS

SOFTWARE-AS-A-SERVICE (SAAS): In SAAS software application is paid on a subscription basis and installed and maintain by the cloud provider's data centre.

PLATFORM-AS-A-SERVICE (PAAS): In PAAS, developers create online applications (apps in short) in platforms provided by the PaaS provider.

INFRASTRUCTURE-AS-A-SERVICE (IAAS): In IaaS service model, organizations use cloud provider's hardware to gain access of computing power and storage capacity This enables them to have control over the infrastructure and run applications in the cloud at a reduced cost.

4. **C, D** (When a network device fails to forward packets, when you require ROMMON access)

Explanation: The advantage of an Out of Band network is that you are separating your user and management traffic and you can take extra steps to secure the management plane. Also, you can configure and manage your devices without the Data Plane even being set up. The disadvantage is the extra cost of setting up a

separate network only for management.

5. **B, C, D** (TACACS uses TCP to communicate with the NAS, it encrypts the entire packet that is delivered to the NAS, it supports per command authentication)

Explanation: TACACS+ encrypts the entire packet body, and also attaches TACACS+ header to the message body. TACACAS ensures reliable delivery between client and server as it uses TCP connection, since it is a cisco proprietary so it have a granular control over cisco's router and switches. TACACS does authentication, authorization and accounting separately, so different methods of controlling AAA functions can be achieved separately.

6. **C, D** (Plain text, MD5)

Explanation: Following are the types of authentication available for OSPF:
a) Null authentication: It means that there is no authentication, which is the default mode on Cisco routers.
b) Clear text authentication: In this method, passwords are traversed in clear text on the network.
c) Cryptographic authentication: It uses the open standard MD5 (Message Digest type 5) encryption.

7. **D, E** (QoS, traffic classification)

Explanation: Control plane policing (CoPP) and Control plane protection (CPPr), provides QoS by filtering out unnecessary traffic towards the router to improve the efficiency of networking device. *It* divides the traffic into three broad categories namely traffic for any physical or logical interface of device, data plane traffic that requires some processing before forwarding and Cisco Express Forwarding error or informational messages.

8. **A, B** (They compare 5-tuples of each incoming packet against configurable rules, they cannot track connections)

Explanation: Stateless firewall monitors network traffic and allow, restrict or block packets based on static values like source and destination addresses. They are not aware of data flows and traffic patterns.

9. **D, E, F** (padding, pad length, next header)

Explanation: Padding is used when the encryption algorithm requires the plain text to be a multiple of some number of bytes. Pad Length is an 8-bit field indicates the number of pad bytes preceding it. Next Header is an 8-bit field that identifies the type of data contained in the Payload Data field.

10. **B, F** (1, 15)

Explanation: When you log in to a new Cisco router, by default you're in user EXEC mode (level 1). In this mode, you can have access to some information about the device. However, you can't make any changes or view the running configuration file.

Typing *enable* directly takes you to level 15, which is privileged EXEC mode. In other words, you can have full access to the router. By default, no password is defined for level 15.

11. **B** (Deny an connection inline)

Explanation: The deny packet inline action is represented as a dropped packet action in the alert. When a deny packet inline occurs for a TCP connection, it is automatically upgraded to a deny connection inline action and seen as a denied flow in the alert. If the IPS denies just one packet, the TCP continues to try to send that same packet again and again, so the IPS denies the entire connection to ensure it never succeeds with the resends.

12. **B** (It provides hardware authentication)

Explanation: Computer programs can use a TPM to authenticate hardware devices, since each TPM chip has a unique and secret RSA key burned in as it is produced. Pushing the security down to the hardware level provides more protection than a software-only solution.

13. **A** (To make sure only authorized parties can manipulate data)

Explanation: Integrity prevents data to be manipulated by unauthorized persons. Data integrity ensures that only authorized parties can modify data.

14. **C** (Provides other company network to your company network)

Explanation: An extranet is a controlled private network that allows access to

partners, vendors and suppliers or an authorized set of customers – normally to a subset of the information accessible from an organization's intranet.

15. **D, E** (It can generate alerts based on the behavior at the desktop level, it can have more restrictive policies than network-based IPS, it can view encrypted files)

Explanation: Host based IPS/IDS is normally deployed for the protection of specific host machine and it works closely to the Operating System Kernel of the host machine. It creates a filtering layer and filters out any malicious application occur at the OS.

16. **D, E, F** (Deny attacker, deny packet, modify packet)

Explanation: A sensor can be deployed either in promiscuous mode or inline mode. In promiscuous mode, the sensor receives a copy of the data for analysis, while the original traffic still makes its way to its ultimate destination. By contrast, a sensor working inline analyzes the traffic live and therefore can actively block the packets before they reach their destination. Consider the article Network Security using Cisco IOS IPS for further details.

17. **C** (Symmetric algorithm)

Explanation: Symmetric Key Cryptography is the oldest and most widely used cryptography technique in the domain of cryptography, symmetric ciphers use the same secret key for the encryption and decryption of data. Most widely used symmetric ciphers are AES and DES.

18. **B** (It queries the active directory server for a specific attribute for the specified user)

Explanation: r. ASA sends RADIUS authentication requests on behalf of VPN users and NPS authenticates them against Active Directory.

19. **B** (Botnet)

Explanation: Botnet is a collection of millions of systems infected with malware under hacker's control in order to launch DDoS attacks. They carry out attacks against the target systems. It usually overwhelms the target system's bandwidth and processing capabilities. These botnets are located in differing geographic locations so

they are difficult to trace.

20. **D** (Education about common Web site vulnerabilities.)

Explanation: The Open Web Application Security Project (OWASP) is a non-profitable group that helps organizations develop, purchase, and maintain software applications that can be trusted.

21. **C** (Cyber warfare)

Explanation: Stuxnet is an extremely dangerous computer worm that exploits multiple unknown zero-day vulnerabilities to infect computers. Cyberwarfare is a virtual conflict initiated as a politically motivated attack on an enemy's computer and information systems.

22. **D** (The supplicant will fail to advance beyond the webauth method)

Explanation: Configured authentication event fail action is to proceed for next method. As per shown configuration, authentication order is mab > dot1x > webauth. If supplicant fails to authenticate for mab or dot1x, it cannot advance beyond webauth method.

23. **C** (9)

Explanation: As shown in the configurations, 9 illegal operations are detected for community name supplied

24. **C** (The time is authoritative, but the NTP process has lost contact with its servers.)

Explanation: The system clock keeps an "authoritative" flag that indicates whether the time is authoritative (believed to be accurate). If the system clock has been set by a timing source, such as system calendar or Network Time Protocol (NTP), the flag is set. If the time is not authoritative, it is used only for display. Until the clock is authoritative and the "authoritative" flag is set, the flag prevents peers from synchronizing to the clock when the peers have invalid times.

Symbol	Description
*	Time is not authoritative.
(blank)	Time is authoritative.
.	Time is authoritative, but NTP is not synchronized.

25. C (ACS Server can be clustered to provide scalability)

Explanation: Cisco Secure ACS 5.5 supports distributed deployment to provide high availability and scalability. A deployment can be composed of multiple Cisco Secure ACS instances that are managed together in a single distributed deployment. One system is designated as primary, and that system accepts configuration changes and propagates them to the secondary instances. For the smallest deployments, one primary and one secondary instance are recommended for redundancy.

26. C (split tunneling)

Explanation: In split tunneling by using *access list* only required traffic goes encrypted over logical tunnel while remaining traffic like internet surfing or local traffic goes out of gateway without any alteration. So by using split-tunneling, end-user can use both *Local Area Network (LAN)* for normal usage and *secure SSL connection* for accessing corporate network at the same time.

27. D (It configures IKE Phase 1)

Explanation: The sequence of commands shown above, is used to define ikev phase 1. Here, crypto isakmp policy with locally assigned number of 1 is defined to use *DES* as encryption algorithm, *MD5* as hashing algorithm, a lifetime period of 3600seconds and DH-group of 2. DH-group needs to be same on both sides as it is internally used by IPSec process for transfer and authenticity of pre-shared key.

28. B (EAP-Fast)

Explanation: Extensible Authentication Protocol (EAP) is used to traverse the authentication information between the supplicant (the Wi-Fi workstation) and the authentication server.
EAP-Fast, it provides flexible authentication via secure tunneling. Here we use PAC

(PROTECTED ACCESS CREDENTIALS) instead of certificates for mutual authentication.

29. **B** (The ISE agent must be installed on the device)

Explanation: ISE is used for secure access management like ACS. It is a single policy control point for entire enterprise including wired and wireless technologies. Before giving access to endpoints or even networking devices itself, ISE checks their identity, location, time, type of device and even health of endpoints to make sure that they comply with company's policy like antivirus, latest service pack and OS updates etc.

30. **C** (Remove the auto command keyword and rest of the arguments from the username admin privilege line.)

Explanation:

The correct sequence of defining a username and password with associated privilege level is:

```
R1(config)# username Admin privilege 15 secret P@$$word:10
```

31. **D** (The secure boot-image command is configured)

Explanation: As router is powered on, rommon mode will appear. As flash does not contain any valid IOS image, dir [filesystem] is used for listing files in a directory.

rommon 1> dir slot1

32. **B** (hair-pinning)

Explanation: Hair-pinning is a method where a packet goes out from an interface but instead of moving towards the internet it makes a hair pin turn, and returns back to the same interface. Usually it seems useless, but it does serves a purpose.

33. **D** (It defines IPSec policy for traffic sourced from 10.10.10.0/24 with a destination of 10.100.100.0/24)

Explanation: A crypto map is a software configuration entity that performs two primary functions:

1. Selects data flows that need security processing.

2. Defines the policy for these flows and the crypto peer to which that traffic needs to go.

A crypto map is applied to an interface. The concept of a crypto map was introduced in classic crypto but was expanded for IPSec.

34. **B** (IPSec phase 1 is established between 10.10.10.2 and 10.1.1.5.)

Explanation: *"show crypto isakmp sa"* command can be used to check the status of security association, in other words the status of IKE Phase 1. It should show the ACTIVE in column named status.

35. **B** (IPSec Phase 2 is established between 10.1.1.1 and 10.1.1.5.)

Explanation: "show crypto ipsec sa" command represents IPsec SAs built between the peers. The encrypted tunnel is built between 10.1.1.1 and 10.1.1.5 for traffic.

36. **D** (It configures the device to begin transmitting the authentication key to other devices at 23:59:00 local time on December 31, 2013 and continue using the key indefinitely)

Explanation: To set the time period during which an authentication key on a key chain is valid to be sent, use the send-lifetime command in key chain key configuration mode. To revert to the default value, use the no form of this command.

- **send-lifetime** *start-time* {**infinite** | *end-time* | **duration** *seconds*}
- **no send-lifetime** [*start-time* {**infinite** | *end-time* | **duration** *seconds*}]

37. **C** (control plane packets)

Explanation: Control packets carry signaling traffic and routing operations for a router. Control packets are generated from a router and are destined for a router. This plane involves the calculation of best routes in the network for traffic, filtering of data i.e. which packet to be sent to the next level or which packet to be discarded, device discovery and many more.

38. **A** (The switch could become the root bridge)

Explanation: In STP attack, an attacker may somehow get the access of switch ports of a network, so that he could place a rogue switch in a network and can manipulate the spanning tree protocol. Here an attacker tries to make his switch a "root switch" and gets the ability to see all traffic that is intended to pass through the root switch.

39. A (MAC Spoofing)

Explanation: MAC Spoofing is a technique of manipulating MAC address to impersonate the legitimate user or launch attack such as Denial-of-Service attack. As we know, MAC address is built-in on Network interface controller which cannot be changed, but some drivers allow to change the MAC address.

40. A (Show ip dhcp snooping binding)

Explanation: "Show ip dhcp snooping binding command displays the DHCP snooping binding database.

41. C (To protect endpoints such as desktops from malicious activities)

Explanation: Personal firewalls also known as desktop firewalls, helps the end-user's personal computers from general attacks from intruders.

42. D (They can protect a system by denying probing requests)

Explanation: Personal firewalls may also provide some level of intrusion detection, allowing the software to terminate or block connectivity where it suspects an intrusion is being attempted. It blocks or alerts the user about all unauthorized inbound or outbound connection attempts.

43. C (Root guard)

Explanation: Root guard is another feature for STP, which prevents less worthy switch from becoming the root bridge.

44. B (The isolated port can communicate only with the promiscuous port.)

Explanation: Following are the different modes of PVLAN:

a) **Promiscuous Mode:** Normally connected to a router, this port is allowed to send and receive frames form any other port on the same VLAN.

b) **Isolated Mode:** As name suggests, devices connected to isolated ports will only communicate with Promiscuous ports.

c) **Community Mode:** Community mode is used for group of users who want communication between them. Community ports can communicate with other community port members and with Promiscuous ports.

45. A (A VLAN hopping attack would be prevented)

Explanation: If we proactively configure both ends of 802.1q trunk with a native VLAN, then all other traffic will be sent with a VLAN tag, but native VLAN's traffic will be sent untagged and this feature can be exploit by an attacker.

Here are some precautionary measures to overcome this problem, discussed above:

a) Disable trunking on all access ports.
b) Disable auto-trunking and enable manual-trunking.
c) Change the native VLAN to a VLAN other than VLAN1.

46. C (A stateful firewall)

Explanation: This is the output of the **show conn protocol tcp** command, which shows the state of all TCP connections through the ASA. These connections can also be seen with the **show conn** command. As we know, state table is maintained by the Stateful firewall.

47. C (Control plane policing can protect the control plane against multicast traffic.)

Explanation: Control plane policing can filter or rate-limit of the any defined traffic in a more granular way.

48. B (Traffic between two interfaces in the same zone is allowed by default.)

Explanation: By default, all traffic between two interfaces in the same zone is always allowed. Traffic from a zone interface to a non-zone interface or from a non-zone interface to a zone interface is always dropped; unless default zones are enabled (default zone is a non-zone interface).

49. D, E (You may set VPN to the lowest security interface to telnet an inside interface, Best practice is to disable Telnet and use SSH)

Explanation: Telnet is a network protocol following a client-server model. It uses TCP channel to provide bidirectional communications between two network devices. One of the oldest communications protocol, Telnet has often been criticized for its lack of security. It does not encrypt communications – many implementations lack a username-password combination for authentication. Telnet has been mostly superseded by the more secure SSH.

50. **C** (Information that is sent over the failover and stateful failover interfaces is sent as clear text by default.)

Explanation: All information sent over the failover and Stateful Failover links is sent in clear text unless you secure the communication with a failover key. If the security appliance is used to terminate VPN tunnels, this information includes any usernames, passwords and pre-shared keys used for establishing the tunnels.

51. **A** (ASA will apply the actions from only the first matching class map it finds for the feature type.)

Explanation: The ASA will apply the actions from only the first matching class map it finds for the feature type. So it is useless to define multiple class maps.

52. **C** (To separate different departments and business units.)

Explanation: Instead of using single hardware firewall for each client connection, service providers can use one high-end firewall and create multiple contexts in it. In this way each client will assume to have a separate piece of hardware as their next hop as traffic will be isolated virtually within on hardware device.

53. **A** (it receives traffic that has already been filtered.)

Explanation: You have just one option of placing an IPS sensor, then placing the sensor just inside the firewall is the best option. Although the inside network is already protected by the firewall, but the users can unintentionally introduce malware into the internal network, where the most critical and confidential data is stored and can be compromised.

54. **C** (A Value that indicates the potential severity of an attack.)

Explanation: You can configure the system to alert you whenever an intrusion event with a specific impact flag occurs. Impact flags help you evaluate the impact an intrusion has on your network by correlating intrusion data, network discovery data, and vulnerability information.

55. **B** (Rate based prevention)

Explanation: Rate-based attack prevention identifies abnormal traffic patterns and attempts to minimize the impact of that traffic on legitimate requests. Rate-based attacks usually have one of the following characteristics:

- Any traffic containing excessive incomplete connections to hosts on the network, indicating a SYN flood attack
- To configure SYN attack detection, see Preventing SYN Attacks.
- Any traffic containing excessive complete connections to hosts on the network, indicating a TCP/IP connection flood attack
- To configure simultaneous connection detection.
- Excessive rule matches in traffic going to a particular destination IP address or addresses or coming from a particular source IP address or addresses.
- To configure source or destination-based dynamic rule states.
- Excessive matches for a particular rule across all traffic.
- To configure rule-based dynamic rule states.

56. **C** (Enable logging at the end of the session.)

Explanation: Logging beginning-of-Connection Events only log information that can be determined in the first packet (or the first few packets, if event generation depends on application or URL identification whereas End-of-connection loggin collects all information in the beginning-of-connection event, plus information determined by examining traffic over the duration of the session, for example, the total amount of data transmitted or the time stamp of the last packet in the connection.

57. **C** (Extract and decode email attachments in client to server traffic.)

Explanation: The SMTP preprocessor instructs the rules engine to normalize SMTP commands. The preprocessor can also extract and decode email attachments in client-to-server traffic and, depending on the software version, extract email file names, addresses, and header data to provide context when displaying intrusion events triggered by SMTP traffic.

58. **A, B** (Configure a proxy server to hide user's local IP addresses, configure a firewall

to use Port address translation)

Explanation: A proxy can keep the internal network structure of a company secret by using network address translation, which can help the security of the internal network. This makes requests from machines and users on the local network anonymous. Proxies can also be combined with firewalls.

59. **C** (Create a whitelist and add the appropriate IP address to allow the traffic)

Explanation: When a blacklist is too broad in scope, or preemptively blocks traffic that you want to further analyze with the rest of access control, you can override a blacklist with a custom whitelist

60. **D** (Every time a new update is available)

Explanation: Vendors keep on updating new version of a particular anti-virus, which is more capable than the previous one, so its best practice to update anti-virus whenever a new update is available.

61. **C** (It blocks access to specific programs)

Explanation: Application blocking, blocks specific applications without disturbing desired applications. Application filtering also offers granular control over some application by blocking features of the Application instead of blocking the complete application. For example, Blocking Chat or Upload option in any application.

62. **D** (Enable URL filtering on the perimeter router and add the URLs you want to block to the router's local URL list.)

Explanation: URL filtering controls the access of URLs by comparing addresses of sites that users are attempting to visit against a database carrying URL list of either permitted or blocked sites. The purpose of URL filtering is to prevent access of the malicious sites, which may introduce malware or threat in the network.

63. **B, C, D** (DHCP-Snooping, anti-spoofing, ACLs)

Explanation: Data plane is responsible for forwarding frames of packets from its ingress to egress interfaces using protocols managed in the control plane. So, protection of data plane is of great importance. Data plane can be made secure by

applying security policies like DHCP-Spoofing, anti-spoofing and by defining ACLs.

64. B (1)

Explanation: The ASA will apply the actions from only the first matching class map it finds for the feature type. So it is useless to define multiple class maps.

65. A (Blocking, listening, learning, forwarding, disabled)

Explanation: Following is the correct order of switch with STP enabled on it.
Blocking, Listening, Learning, Forwarding, Disabled

66. C (Minimizing risk)

Explanation: Due to the increasing rate of network attacks, companies make security policies which includes the placement of relevant devices, relevant softwares and rules to allow or deny certain traffic.

67. C (0.0.0.31)

Explanation: Wild card associate with the subnet of /27 means there are 5 host bits as IPv4 address is of 32bits.

		128	64	32	16	8	4	2	1
Lowest address	0.0.0.0	0	0	0	0	0	0	0	0
Highest address	0.0.0.31	0	0	0	1	1	1	1	1

68. A, B, C (Reflexive access lists support UDP sessions, Reflexive access lists support TCP sessions, Reflexive access can be attached to extended named IP ACLs)

Explanation: Reflexive access lists provides a better level of security against spoofing and certain denial-of-service attacks. Reflexive access lists are almost similar in many ways to other access lists. Reflexive access list works on condition statements that

define criteria for permitting or denying IP packets. These entries are evaluated in order, and when a match occurs, no more entries are evaluated. A reflexive access list is triggered whenever a new IP upper-layer session such as TCP or UDP is initiated.

69. **B, C, D** (Resetting the TCP connection, requesting host blocking, requesting connection blocking)

Explanation: There are three types of blocks:

Host block — Blocks all traffic from a given IP address.

Connection block — Blocks traffic from a given source IP address to a given destination IP address and destination port.

Network block — Blocks all traffic from a given network.

70. **B** (Health and performance monitor)

Explanation: Cisco Security Manager enables consistent policy enforcement and rapid troubleshooting of security events, offering summarized reports of network health across the security deployment. By using CSM, organizations can scale and manage a wide range of Cisco security devices with improved visibility.

71. **B, C** (Start stop, stop only)

Explanation: AAA Accounting uses stop-only keyword to send a "stop" record accounting notice at the end of the requested user process and it uses the start-stop keyword, so that RADIUS or TACACS+ sends a "start" accounting notice at the beginning of the requested process and a "stop" accounting notice at the end of the process. Accounting is stored only on the RADIUS or TACACS+ server. The none keyword disables accounting services for the specified line or interface.

72. **C** (crypto key generate RSA)

Explanation: Here is the sequence of commands for enabling SSH on a router:

Set the domain name and RSA for SSH

R1(config)# `ip domain name IPSpecialist.net`

R1(config)# `crypto key generate rsa general-keys modulus 1024`

Set the SSH version to 2

```
R1(config)# ip ssh version 2
```

73. E (SCP)

Explanation: SCP is secure copy protocol used for transferring files between client and server machines. SCP uses SSH for data transfer and authentication hence adds both authenticity and confidentiality during whole transaction. SCP allows users with appropriate authorization level to securely copy any file from that exists in the Cisco IOS File System.

74. C (The self-zone)

Explanation: In Cisco devices, traffic to the self-zone either in ingress direction or egress direction is permitted by default. However, filtering can be done on traffic directed towards the router by creating a zone pair (involving the self-zone) and applying policy to it.

75. C, D (The Internet Key Exchange protocol establishes security associations, the internet key exchange protocol is responsible for mutual authentication)

Explanation: The first step of initiation of VPN between two peers is known as **Internet Key Exchange (IKE)** phase 1 tunnel. This phase is not used for sending encrypted user traffic. Instead, it is used for securing the management traffic related to VPN connection between two peers. After successful establishment of IKE phase1 tunnel, a second tunnel known as IKE phase 2 tunnel is established, again with mutual agreement, to secure the end user IP traffic.

76. C (FD00::/8)

Explanation: Unique local IPv6 addresses are not meant to be routed outside their domain and works as a private address of IPv4. Unique local IPv6 addresses range begin with **FD00::/8**.

77. A (Router is a new device on which the AAA new model command must be applied before continuing)

Explanation:

```
Router(config)# aaa new-model
```

Enables the AAA access control model. If router is not pre-configured, administrator must have to issue the command to enable AAA model.

78. C (STP loop may occur)

Explanation: In order to prevent VLAN hopping attack change the native VLAN to a VLAN other than VLAN1. But native VLAN should be configured with the same number on both the ends between switches, otherwise loops can occur.

79. B (Direction of the access group)

Explanation: Only one access list per interface, per protocol, and per direction is allowed. Inbound access lists process packets before the packets are routed to an outbound interface. Outbound access lists process packets before they leave the device.

80. A (UDP 4500)

Explanation: IKE uses port UDP 4500 for NAT traversal.

81. A, B, C (IPSec transport mode supports unicast, IPSec transport mode encrypts only payload, IPSec transport mode is used between end stations)

Explanation: In transport mode, IPSec VPN secures the data field or payload of originating IP traffic by using encryption, hashing or both. New IPSec headers encapsulate only payload field while the original IP headers remain unchanged. Tunnel mode is used when original IP packets are source and destination address of secure IPSec peers. For example, securing the management traffic of router is a perfect example of IPSec VPN implementation using transport mode.

82. A (no switchport)

Explanation: In order to enable a layer 2 interface to work as a Layer 3 routed interface, use the following commands:

switch(config)# interface ethernet 1

switch(config-if)# no switchport

switch(config-if)#

In order to enable a layer 3 interface to work as a Layer 2 routed interface, use the

following commands:

switch(config)# interface ethernet 1

switch(config-if)# switchport

83. B (Asset)

Explanation: An **Asset** is something which is directly or indirectly related to the revenue of an organization.

84. D (Host based IPS)

Explanation: Host based IPS/IDS is normally deployed for the protection of specific host machine and it works closely to the Operating System Kernel of the host machine. It creates a filtering layer and filters out any malicious application occur at the OS.

85. A (IP OSPF authentication message-digest)

Explanation: In order enable OSPF authentication use message digest based password on multi-access network, use the following commands:

R1(config)#interface FastEthernet 0/0

R1(config-if)#ip ospf authentication message-digest

86. B (catalyst1(config)#username user1 privilege 0 secret us1pass)

Explanation: Cisco IOS allows users to make different privilege levels from Level 1 to Level 15, it eases the management of network staff itself. By default, privilege level 15 is set on cisco devices but level 15 is of great concern regarding the security of device, having access of all configurations to all users is not a good approach of securing network. There are five commands associated with privilege level 0: disable, enable, exit, help, and logout.

87. C (Area 20 authentication message-digest)

Explanation: Following sequence of commands will be used for OSPF's MD5 authentication:

R3(config)#interface FastEthernet 0/0

R3(config-if)#ip ospf authentication message-digest

R3(config-if)#ip ospf authentication-key P@$$word:10

88. B, C (Dynamic NAT, Static NAT)

Explanation:

Dynamic NAT: You cannot use an inline address; you must configure a network object or group.

Dynamic PAT: Instead of using an object, you can optionally configure an inline host address or specify the interface address. If you use an object, the object or group cannot contain a subnet; the object must define a host, or for a PAT pool, a range; the group (for a PAT pool) can include hosts and ranges.

Static NAT or Static NAT with port translation: If you use an object, the object or group can contain a host, range, or subnet.   Instead of using an object, you can configure an inline address or specify the interface address (for static NAT-with-port-translation).

Identity NAT: Instead of using an object, you can configure an inline address. If you use an object, the object must match the real addresses you want to translate.

89. A (Promiscuous mode)

Explanation: Ports assigned to private VLAN will have one of the following types:

a) **Promiscuous Mode:** Normally connected to a router, this port is allowed to send and receive frames form any other port on the same VLAN.

b) **Isolated Mode:** As name suggests, devices connected to isolated ports will only communicate with Promiscuous ports.

c) **Community Mode:** Community mode is used for group of users who want communication between them. Community ports can communicate with other community port members and with Promiscuous ports.

90. C, D (Secure boot-config, secure boot-image)

Explanation:

Following command is used for IOS image secure backup.

Router(config)# secure boot-image

Similarly following command is used for secure configuration backup in persistent

storage.

Router(config)# secure boot-config

91. **A, B** (Gaining access to server room by posing as IT, watching other user put in username and password)

Explanation: Social Engineering in Information Security refers to the technique of psychological manipulation. This trick is used to gather information from different social networking and other platforms from people for fraud, hacking and getting information for being close to the target.

92. **B** (Integrity)

Explanation: We do not want our data to be accessible or manipulated by some unauthorized persons. Data integrity ensures that only authorized parties can modify data. Integrity ensures the information received at the recipient's end is exactly the information sent originally by the sender.

93. **B** (Denial of service)

Explanation: TCP SYN flood or SYN flood attack is a type of Distributed Denial of Service (DDoS) attack that exploits part of the normal TCP three-way handshake to achieve resources of the targeted server and make it unresponsive for the legitimate users.

94. A (Anomaly based IPS/IDS)

Explanation: Anomaly Based IDS/IPS

In this type a baseline is created for the specific kind of traffic. For example, after analyzing the traffic, it is noticed that 30 half open TCP sessions are created every minute. After deciding the baseline, say 35 half open TCP connections in a minute. Consider a scenario where, the number of half open TCP connected have increased up to 150 then IPS will drop the extra half open connections and will generate alert for it based on the decided anomaly.

95. B (show crypto isakmp sa)

Explanation: *"show crypto isakmp sa"* command can be used to check the status of security association, in other words the status of IKE Phase 1. It should show the ACTIVE in column named status.

96. A (Proxy)

Explanation: A proxy-based firewall acts as an intermediary wall between the requested data by the end users and the destination servers. The proxy filters all network traffic and will block or allow traffic based on its rule set transparently.

97. B (Debugging)

Explanation: Here is the table representing the levels of syslog:

Emergencies	0	System is unusable
Alerts	1	Immediate Action needed
Critical	2	Critical Condition
Errors	3	Error Condition
Warnings	4	Warning Condition
Notifications	5	Normal but require attention
Informational	6	Informational messages
Debugging	7	Debugging messages with maximum details depending on number of processes for which debugging is enabled

98. A (Phishing)

Explanation: phishing tries to get login credentials by manipulating the end-user by presenting different links which looks legitimate, for example presenting fake social web pages. Sometimes attacker gather some important information of targeted employees of specific organization and then generate more directed phishing attacks.

99. A (Local mirroring over layer 2)

Explanation: The Switched Port Analyzer (SPAN) or port mirroring is a feature for

Cisco switches, its function is to send copies of the frame entering a port to the IDS/IPS sensor. SPAN.

100.   C (Only the time source)

Explanation: Cisco routers can be set to be the NTP Clients of publically available NTP servers, we can set a single device in network infrastructure to be NTP server and all the devices will synchronize their time according to the NTP server.

101. C (Web security appliance)

Explanation: Additional precautionary steps to protect critical information from getting effected by malwares on web can be encounter by Cisco's Cloud based Web Security (CWS) along with Cisco Web Security Appliance (WSA). It helps in this regard by providing continuous monitoring and detection of latest malware and other threats.

102.   B (A private VLAN partitions the layer 2 broadcast domain of a VLAN into subdomains)

Explanation: A private VLAN divides a VLAN into subdomains, making you to isolate the ports on the switch from each other. A subdomain consists of a primary VLAN and one or more secondary VLANs.

103.   B (MD5)

Explanation: MD5 hashes are used to ensure the data integrity of files. Because the MD5 hash algorithm always produces the same output for the same given input, users can compare a hash of the source file with a newly created hash of the destination file to check that it is unaltered and unmodified.

104.   C (Unicast Reverse Path Forwarding)

Explanation: The Unicast Reverse Path Forwarding feature limits the malicious traffic on a network. This feature enables devices to verify the reachability of the source address in packets that are being forwarded and limit the appearance of spoofed or malformed addresses on a network. If the source IP address is not valid, Unicast Reverse Path Forwarding (RPF) discards the packet.

105. **B** (Denial of service)

Explanation: Denial-of-Service (DoS) is a type of attack in which service offered by a system or a network is denied. Services may either be denied, reduced the functionality or prevent the access to the resources even to the legitimate users.

106. **C** (Dynamic port security)

Explanation: Dynamic Port Security is used to bind the MAC address of known devices to the physical ports and violation action is also defined.

107. **B** (Inline behind the internet router and firewall)

Explanation: When the senor is placed in line with the network i.e. the common in/out of specific network segment terminates on a hardware or logical interface of a sensor and goes out from another hardware or logical interface of sensor, then every single packet will be analyzed and pass through sensor only if it does not contain anything malicious. By dropping the malicious traffic, the trusted network or a segment of it can be protected from known threats and attacks.

108. **A, B** (The user will be prompted to authenticate using the enable password, authentication attempts to the router will be denied)

Explanation: To set authentication, authorization, and accounting (AAA) authentication at login, use the aaa authentication login command in global configuration mode. To disable AAA authentication, use the no form of this command.

```
aaa authentication login default group tacacs+ enable
```

enable: Uses the enable password for authentication.

group tacacs+: Uses the list of all TACACS+ servers for authentication.

109. **A** (SDEE)

Explanation: The Security Device Event Exchange (SDEE) protocol is used to communicate the events generated by security devices. The SDEE client establishes a session with the server by successfully authenticating with that server. Once the

session gets authenticated, a session cookie or session ID is assigned to the client, which will be attached with all future requests.

110. **B** (STP elects the root bridge)

Explanation: Spanning tree protocol (STP) is a layer 2 technology and its main function is to make a loop free network at Layer 2 of TCP/IP stack. STP do this by selecting a *Root Bridge* in a network and making a loop free network with respect to *Root Bridge*. Like every other protocol, selecting root bridge is done by comparing some parameters of every single layer 2 device in a network.

111. **B** (Static NAT)

Explanation: In transparent mode, no IP address is assigned to an interface. However, name and security level is assigned to an interface to make it operational. So entries should be manually entered to make NATing work.

112. **C, D** (The hash, the key)

Explanation: Hash-based Message Authentication Code (HMAC) is a code that authenticates a message. It uses a cryptographic key in conjunction with a hash function.

113. **B** (5 seconds)

Explanation: The default timeout interval during which a router waits for responses from a TACACS server before declaring a timeout failure is 5 seconds.

114. **A, C** (DHCP Snooping, dynamic ARP inspection)

Explanation: DHCP Snooping is a security feature designed by Cisco, to mitigate the issues created by rogue DHCP servers. It is a security feature that behaves like a firewall between trusted DHCP servers and untrusted hosts. DHCP snooping validates the DHCP messages either received from the legitimate source or from an untrusted source and filters out invalid messages.

Dynamic *ARP* inspection helps to mitigate the common attack of *ARP* spoofing in which an attacker tries to reply *ARP* requests and sends its own *MAC* address and results in man-in-the-middle attacks.

115. **B, C, D** (Extended access lists should be placed as near as possible to the source, Standard access lists should be placed as near as possible to the destination, Standard access lists filter on the source address)

Explanation: Standard access lists are placed closest to the destination because the of the lack of feature to specify the destination in the standard ACL statements. This results in ALL traffic originating from that source to ANY destination getting dropped. Since an Extended Access Control List (ACL) can filter the IP datagram packet based on the destination IP address, it must be placed on the router which is near to the source network/host. If we place the Extended Access Control List (ACL) near to destination, the unwanted traffic may consume the bandwidth till destination, and the the unwanted traffic will get filtered finally near destination.

116. **D, E** (CCPr, CoPP)

Explanation: Control Plane Policing (CoPP) is implemented which identify specific traffic type and limits its rate that is reaching the control plane of device. Another great feature to secure the control plane is the use of **Control Plane Protection (CPPr)** features. *CPPr* gives granular control over the traffic entering the control plane of device.

117. **B** (Reconnaissance)

Explanation: Reconnaissance is an initial preparing phase for the attacker to get ready for an attack by gathering the information about the target before launching an attack using different tools and techniques. Gathering of information about the target makes it easier for an attacker, even on a large scale. Similarly, in large scale, it helps to identify the target range.

118. **A, E** (SSH, HTTPS)

Explanation: Secure shell (SHH), let you to remotely access another system or device securely.

HTTP over SSL (HTTPS) provides additional protocol **for** security **to HTTP.**

119. **B, C** (Double tagging, switch spoofing)

Explanation:

801.q Double tagging: An attacker can Spoof DTP messages from the attacking host

to cause the switch to enter trunking mode. Here, he applies double tagging the first tag comprises of native VLAN to bypass trunking and other tag is of victim's VLAN to reach the victim. So that, the attacker can send traffic tagged with the target VLAN, and the switch simply delivers the packets to the destination.

Switch Spoofing: An attacker may Introduce a rogue switch and enable trunking. Then attacker can then get all the VLANs on the rogue switch from the victim's switch.

120. **B, C** (collecting and archiving syslog data, alerting administrators to security events in real time)

Explanation: Security Information Management(SIM) and Security Event Management(SEM) are evolved to form a byproduct by the name of Security Information and Event Management (SIEM). In Network security, SIEM technology allows you to get real-time visibility of all activities, threats and risks in your system, network, database and application.

- o It provides a comprehensive and centralized view of an IT infrastructure.
- o It provides real-time analysis of logs and security alerts generated by network hardware or application.
- o It saves data for the long time, so the organizations can have a detailed report of incident.
- o SIEM provides details on the Cause of suspicious activity, which leads you to know "How that event occurred", "Who is associated with that event", "Was the user authorized for doing this", etc.

121. **B, C, D** (access, core, distribution)

Explanation: There are the following layers of typical hierarchical network design:

- • Access layer: Provides user direct access to the network
- • Distribution layer: Provides policy-based connectivity amongst the network devices
- • Core layer: Provides fast transport between distribution switches of the network

122. **D, E, F** (RADIUS uses UDP to communicate with the NAS, RADIUS encrypts only the password field in an authentication packet, RADIUS authenticates and authorizes simultaneously, causing fewer packets to be transmitted.)

Explanation: Here is the table indicating the differences between RADIUS and

TACACS:

	TACACS+	RADIUS
L4 Protocol	TCP port 49.	UDP ports. 1812/1645 for authentication 1813/1646 for accounting.
Encryption	Encrypts full payload of each packet	Encrypts only passwords.
Observations	Proprietary to Cisco, very granular control over authorization, separate implementation of AAA.	Open Standard, robust, great accounting features, less granular authorization control. Another protocol named DIAMETER may replace RADIUS in near future with enhanced capabilities.
Primary use	Device administration	Network access

123.   **D, E, F** (They can modify traffic in transit, they are used to perform man-in-the-middle attacks, they use ARP poisoning.)

Explanation: In DHCP spoofing attack, the attacker places a rogue DHCP server on the network. As clients get connected to the network and request an IP address from a DHCP pool and if the device gets a response from the rogue server first, the rogue server will assign any address and other information to the client. Thus, making the attacker to steal the information almost invisibly.

124.   **A** (confidentiality)

Explanation: Confidentiality means that only authorized persons can discover our infrastructure's digital resources. It also implies that unauthorized persons should not have any access or disclosure of the data.

125.   **B** (Phishing)

Explanation: Phishing tries to get login credentials by manipulating the end-user by presenting different links which looks legitimate, for example presenting fake social web pages.

126.   **B** (URL Categorization)

Explanation: URL Categorization controls the user access to specific website

category. This feature enables networking device to filter web traffic by using a categorization database.

127.   **A, B, C** (It defines the rules and policies to allow or block specific application or data, It blocks hidden malware in encrypted SSL/TLS traffic, It detects and blocks Intrusion attempts from an attacker)

Explanation: TLS/SSL decryption performs the following actions:

a) It blocks hidden malware in encrypted SSL/TLS traffic

b) It detects and blocks Intrusion attempts from an attacker

c) It restricts confidential data from loss, hence provides Data Loss Prevention (DLP)

d) It defines the rules and policies to allow or block specific application or data

e) It monitors outgoing data

128.   **E** (All of the above)

Explanation: Web based attacks includes cross site scripting (XSS), SQL injection, file inclusion, cross site forgery etc.

129.   **B** (Malware is unwanted software that is harmful or destructive)

Explanation: The term **Malware** refers to a variety of hostile or intrusive software including computer viruses, worms, Trojan horses, ransomware, spyware, adware, scareware, and other malicious programs. It can take the form of executable code, scripts, active content, and other software.

130.   **B** (public/private key pair)

Explanation: In Asymmetric Key Cryptography, two keys are used. One key is publically known to everyone while one key is kept secret and is used to encrypt the data by sender hence it is also called Public Key cryptography. Each sender uses its own secret key (also known as private key) for encrypting its data before sending. The receiver uses the respective public key of sender to decrypt the data.

131. **C** (Use the test aaa command.)

Explanation: To associate a dialed number identification service (DNIS) or calling line identification (CLID) user profile with the record that is sent to the RADIUS server or to manually test load-balancing server status, use the test aaa group command in privileged EXEC mode.

132.   **C** (It encrypts the exchange using the server certificate)

Explanation: EAP-PEAP, it is a protected extensible authentication protocol. It provides a method to traverse authentication data (like password based protocols, via 802.11 networks) securely. PEAP achieves this by using tunneling between PEAP clients and authentication server.

133.**B** (it allows multiple credentials to be passed in a single EAP exchange.)

Explanation: EAP-Fast, it provides flexible authentication via secure tunneling. Here we use PAC (PROTECTED ACCESS CREDENTIALS) instead of certificates for mutual authentication.

134.   **D** (always-on)

Explanation: *Always on* is one of the features used with *Cisco's AnyConnect* Client software for SSL based VPN. When enabled, end-user will not be able to access public network resources like internet surfing until and unless a VPN session is active. This feature allows an automatic establishment of VPN session as user logs in the computer and remain open until user logs out.

135.   **B** (NAT)

Explanation: Private addresses are used to allow devices to communicate with in an organization locally. However, private IPv4 addresses are not routable over the Internet.

136.   **D** (Edit the crypto keys on R1 and R2 to match.)

Explanation: Difference in keys configured on R1 and R2 is preventing to establish a connection.

137.   **A** (It merges authentication and encryption methods to protect traffic that

matches an ACL)

Explanation: The command shows the definition of *IPSEC-TRANSFORMSET* named transform-set with *DES* and *MD5* as encryption and hashing algorithms respectively. It's a significant name and can be defined suitable to one's understanding. By default, Tunnel mode is selected for IPSec VPN connection type. Tunnel mode means whole IP packet (including IP header) will be encapsulated with new IP header by IPSec.

138.   **B** (Each privilege level supports the commands at its own level and all levels below it.)

Explanation: We set custom privilege levels and assign them to different users and groups depending on the role of their job. We can custom privilege levels in between 1 and 15. The user with level 1 will not be able to make changes in configuration and the user with level 15 can do anything from configuration to deleting some data.

139.   **C** (Process ID)

Explanation: The process ID is the ID of the OSPF process to which the interface belongs.

The process ID is local to the router, and two OSPF neighboring routers can have different OSPF process IDs.

140.   **B** (Access control lists)

Explanation: Control Plane Policing can be implemented by granular use of **Access Control Lists (ACLs)** and **logging feature** of device.

141. **D** (MAC Flooding)

Explanation: MAC table helps the switch to track of where to send the traffic for specific learned MAC address. MAC address table is also stored in Random Access Memory (RAM) and CPU allocates specific memory space for it along with other programs, which require CPU as well as RAM. Kali Linux or Back Track have tools, generates random MAC addresses. By using such tools, MAC address table of layer 2 device will overflow within minutes. The next frame being hit on any interface of layer 2 device will result in broadcast to all ports and switch may start behaving as if a hub, which did not, had the memory space to store ARP entries.

142.   **B** (It may be susceptible to a VLAN hoping attack.)

Explanation: By default, VLAN 1 is referred to as native VLAN. Usually, in Cisco's LAN connection the switch left the native VLAN untagged on 802.1Q trunk ports. The practice of sending native VLAN's packet untagged can lead your network towards a security vulnerability.

143.   **C** (Inline)

Explanation: When the senor is placed in line with the network i.e. the common in/out of specific network segment terminates on a hardware or logical interface of a sensor and goes out from another hardware or logical interface of sensor, then every single packet will be analysed and pass through sensor only if it does not contain anything malicious. By dropping the malicious traffic, the trusted network or a segment of it can be protected from known threats and attacks. This is the basic working of Intrusion Prevention System (IPS).

144.   **A** (Use a third-party system to perform penetration testing.)

Explanation: A false negative is a situation when something malicious is introduced in a network and IPS/IDS sensor could not generate any alert due to some unforeseen reasons. In this case, some extra tools and techniques like penetration testing is required to get update related to such situations like Syslog messages from routers.

145.   **C** (To configure an event action that takes place when a signature is triggered)

Explanation: The IPS event action rules dictate the actions that the sensor performs when an event occurs. Although each signature is configured with specific actions that should be taken, the actual actions performed also depend on other factors.

146.   **C** (File reputationn)

Explanation: File reputation gets the information from Cisco cloud based intelligence service named as TALOS, for a reputation verdict of an IP or traffic. Here the malicious traffic will automatically be blocked. File reputation service gets updated after every 3 to 5 minutes.

147.   **C** (It blocks known vulnerabilities without patching applications)

Explanation: Web application filtering protects your web or mobile applications from

being compromised and prevents data from breaching. Web application filtering can be done by either defining filtering policy or by using web application firewall (WAF).

148. A (It sends the traffic through a file policy.)

Explanation: A file policy is a set of configurations that the system uses to perform advanced malware protection and file control, as part of your overall access control configuration. You can associate a single file policy with an access control rule whose action is Allow, Interactive Block, or Interactive Block with reset.

149. C (STP BPDU guard)

Explanation: If an attacker gets a chance to connect his switch to the switch segment of STP and sends illegal BPDU packets stating itself to have best BPDU guard, all switches will align themselves according to it. In order to prevent this situation, BPDU guard feature must be enabled on access ports, which disables the port in case of any BPDU packet seen in inbound direction. Once a port is disabled due to BPDU violation, it will show error-disabled state.

150. C, E (51,50)

Explanation: There are two primary protocols used with IPsec are AH and ESP:
   a) AH is protocol number 51 and provides data authentication and integrity for IP packets that are exchanged between the peers.
   b) ESP, which is protocol number 50, performs packet encryption.

151. B (False positive)

Explanation: A false positive is a situation when sensor generates an alert about the traffic which is not malicious, but requires serious attention as long as security is concerned. False positive can be easily identified, as immediate alerts are generated for this and they can be easily viewed.

152. C (Attack severity Ratings)

Explanation:

Attack Severity Rating (ASR)	It is also the part of digital signature and it determines the critical level of an attack.

153. **B** (zero-day attack)

Explanation: A **zero-day attack** or zero-day threat is an attack that exploits the weakness of any software that are unknown by the software vendor. An attacker can launch attack before the vendor release any patch of this vulnerability and the network can be compromised.

154. **A** (it introduces delay because every packet is analyzed before forwarded to destination.)

Explanation: IPS responds immediately to an attack and does not allow any malicious traffic to bypass network device, but it introduces delay in a network as it analyzes each and every packet that passes through an interface.

155. **D** (All of the above)

Explanation: IPS provides network protection by preventing an attack to reach its destination, by enforcing policies, by controlling access to resources and by hardening networking devices.

156. **B** (fail open mode)

Explanation: If 'fail-open' mode is used, the good and malicious traffic will be allowed in case of any kind of failure within IPS sensor.

If 'fail-close' mode is configured, the whole IP traffic will be dropped in case of sensor's failure.

157. **B** (Dynamic Blacklisting)

Explanation: IPS helps you to dynamically create a blacklist, with the help of Cisco Collective Security Intelligence Team "Talos" (http://www.talosintel.com/).

It dynamically downloads a collection of IP addresses at regular intervals, that have a poor reputation in networking environment.

158. **B** (Whitelisting)

Explanation: **Whitelisting** is just the opposite of blacklisting, here you allow or permit IP address or traffic of your own choice.

Blacklisting and whitelisting are widely used for security solutions, including IPS, web

security, email security, and firewall.

159. **A, B, C** (Predefined URL categories, Custom URL categories, Dynamic content analysis)

Explanation: For providing more granular web security, URL filtering can be performed. URL filtering controls the access of URLs by comparing addresses of sites that users are attempting to visit against a database carrying URL list of either permitted or blocked sites. Here are some actions associated with the URL filtering policy:

- **Blocked-** This action can be applied to the distracting websites like local news, social media, or to the sites known to have various forms of malware.
- **Allowed-** This action can be applied to websites relevant to the organization and its workflow.
- **Blocked or allowed URL categories-** When actions are applied by the category not on a site-by-site basis. This might include categories for malware or phishing sites, innocent but distracting sites, or questionable sites.

160. **C, D** (DHCP Spoofing, MAC address spoofing)

Explanation: In DHCP spoofing attack, the attacker places a rogue DHCP server on the network. As clients get connected to the network and request an IP address from a DHCP pool and if the device gets a response from the rogue server first, the rogue server will assign any address and other information to the client. Thus, making the attacker to steal the information almost invisibly.

This masking process of MAC address is known as MAC Spoofing. Attacker sniffs the MAC address of users which are active on switch ports and duplicate the MAC address. Duplicating the MAC can intercept the traffic and traffic destined to the legitimate user may direct to the attacker.

161. **C, D** (SHA, MD5)

Explanation: MD5 and SHA hashes are used to ensure the data integrity of files. Because the MD5 hash algorithm always produces the same output for the same given input, users can compare a hash of the source file with a newly created hash of the destination file to check that it is unaltered and unmodified.

162. **C** (Main mode)

Explanation: Main mode and aggressive mode are two modes of IKE Phase 1.

163. **D** (Ensuring that the native VLAN of the trunk ports is different from the native VLAN of the user ports)

Explanation: Here are some precautionary measures to overcome vlan hpping and double tagging attack:

- Disable trunking on all access ports.
- Disable auto-trunking and enable manual-trunking.
- Change the native VLAN to a VLAN other than VLAN1.
- Tag the native VLAN traffic in order to prevent against 802.1Q double-tagging attack to exploit network vulnerability.
- Native VLAN of the trunk ports is different from the native VLAN of the users port.

164. **A, B, C** (A firewall can introduce a performance bottleneck, if a system in a security zone is compromised a firewall can help to contain the attack within that zone, a firewall can prevent undesired access to a network security zone.)

Explanation: A firewall is a crucial component of securing your network and is designed to address the issues of data integrity or traffic authentication (via stateful packet inspection) and confidentiality of your internal network (via NAT). Your network gains these benefits from a firewall by receiving all transmitted traffic through the firewall. Your network gains these benefits from a firewall by receiving all transmitted traffic through the firewall. The importance of including a firewall in your security strategy is apparent; however, firewalls do have the following limitations:

- A firewall cannot prevent users or attackers with modems from dialing in to or out of the internal network, thus bypassing the firewall and its protection completely.
- Firewalls cannot enforce your password policy or prevent misuse of passwords. Your password policy is crucial in this area because it outlines acceptable conduct and sets the ramifications of noncompliance.
- Firewalls are ineffective against nontechnical security risks such as social engineering, as discussed in Chapter 1, "There Be Hackers Here."

- Firewalls cannot stop internal users from accessing websites with malicious code, making user education critical.
- Firewalls cannot protect you from poor decisions.
- Firewalls cannot protect you when your security policy is too lax.

165.   B (Man-in-the-middle-attack)

Explanation: To implement man in the middle attack at Layer 3, attacker can introduce a rouge router in network and make sure that other routers see this router as preferred path for destination routes. To stop such kind of attacks, we can use authentication for routing protocols used in network, use Access Lists to permit only required traffic etc.

166.   A (Signature-based inspection)

Explanation: A signature-based inspection checks for some specific string or behavior in a single packet or stream of packets to detect the anomaly. Cisco IPS/IDS modules and next generation firewalls come up with the preloaded digital signatures which can be used to mitigate already discovered attacks.

167.   B (IPSec)

Explanation: A site to site VPN securely connects two or more sites that wants to connect together over the internet. For examples, a corporate office wants to connect to its head office or there are multiple branches wants to connect with each other. This is referred to as site-to-site VPN. Site-to-site VPN usually use IPSEC as a VPN technology.

168.   B (A network-scanning technique that indicates the number of live hosts in a range of IP addresses.)

Explanation: A ping sweep is a network-scanning tool to determine the range of IP addresses mapped with live hosts. This utility is popularly used to encounter reconnaissance attack to gather information about live hosts in a network.

169.   C, E, F (Confidentiality, Integrity & Availability)

Explanation: There are three main components of information security:

a) Confidentiality: makes sure that only authorized users can see and tamper data. It provides encryption to encrypt and hide data.

b) Integrity: makes sure that the data remains un-tampered during transit.

c) Availability: makes sure that the data remains available for authorized users.

170.   **A, C, D** (It provides a comprehensive and centralized view of an IT infrastructure, It provides real-time analysis of logs and security alerts generated by network hardware or application, It saves data for the long time, so the organizations can have a detailed report of incident)

Explanation: Security Information Management (SIM) and Security Event Management (SEM) are evolved to form a by-product by the name of Security Information and Event Management (SIEM). In Network security, SIEM technology allows you to get real-time visibility of all activities, threats and risks in your system, network, database and application.

o   It provides a comprehensive and centralized view of an IT infrastructure.

o   It provides real-time analysis of logs and security alerts generated by network hardware or application.

o   It saves data for the long time, so the organizations can have a detailed report of an incident.

o   SIEM provides details on the Cause of suspicious activity, which leads you to know "How that event occurred?", "Who is associated with that event?", "Was the user authorized for doing this?", etc.

171. **A** (Common Vulnerabilities and Exposures (CVE))

Explanation: Cisco and other security vendors have created databases known as *The Common Vulnerabilities and Exposures (CVE)* that categorizes the threats over the internet. It can be searched via any search engine available today.

172.   **A** (Denial-of-Service Attack)

Explanation: Denial-of-Service (DOS) attack is an availability attack intended to downgrade or deny the targeted service or application.

173.   **A, C, D** (Social Engineering, Reconnaissance & Pharming)

Explanation: Information gathering is a pre-attack phase, which includes the collection of information about a target using different techniques. An attacker may use different tools, commands for extracting information. Popular methods for gathering information are:

- Social Engineering
- Reconnaissance
- Phishing and Pharming

174. **A** (DoS attack)

Explanation: Denial-of-Service (DoS) is a type of attack in which services offered by a system or a network is denied. Services may either be denied, reduced the functionality or prevent the access to the resources even to the legitimate users. There are several techniques to perform DoS attack such as generating a large number of requests to the target system for service.

175. **B, D** (Intrusion Prevention System & Anti-Spoofing Technologies)

Explanation: The key components to deal with DoS attacks are firewalls and IPSec, but anti-virus software is frequently used to protect a system from viruses and encryption help in mitigating man-in-the-middle attack and reconnaissance.

176. **C** (Man-in-the-Middle)

Explanation: Man-In-The-Middle attack can be explained as a user communicating with another user, or server and attacker inserting himself in between the conversation by sniffing the packets and generating MITM or Replay traffic.

177. **C** (Malicious software, which is designed to disguise itself misleading users of its true intent)

Explanation: Trojan is malicious software, which disguise itself in some legitimate application like free screen saver, free anti-virus cracker, once it is downloaded it will attack end-users.

178. **D** (A worm is a self-replicating malware, which infects system, files or programs)

Explanation: A worm is a self-replicating malware, which infects system, files or programs. They are the special type of viruses that spread over the network thus infecting multiple vulnerable systems.

179. **B** (Reconnaissance)

Explanation: Reconnaissance is an initial preparing phase for the attacker to get ready for an attack by gathering the information about the target before launching an attack using different tools and techniques.

180. **A** (Ransomware)

Explanation: Ransomware is malicious software, which is designed to encrypt user's data, then hackers demand ransom payment to decrypt the respective data.

181. **B** (Brute-Force Attack)

Explanation: A brute force attack is a trial-and-error method used to exploit information such as a user password or Personal Identification Number (PIN). In this attack, automated software is used to generate a large number of consecutive guesses as to the value of the desired data. Brute force attacks may be used by criminals to crack encrypted data, or by security analysts to test an organization's network security.

182. **A** (Campus Area Network)

Explanation: Campus Area Network is a type of network topology where multiple LANs are interconnected but it is not expanded as Wide Area Network (WAN) or Metropolitan Area Network (MAN). CAN provides connectivity and services amongst all the branches and end-users of a geographically separated organization like different campuses of a university, multiple offices of an organization etc.

183. **B** (Cryptography)

Explanation: Cryptography is a technique of encrypting the clear text data into a scrambled code. This encrypted data is sent over public or private network towards a destination to ensure the confidentiality.

184. **C** (Symmetric Key Cryptography)

Explanation: Symmetric Key Cryptography is the oldest and most widely used

cryptography technique in the domain of cryptography; symmetric ciphers use the same secret key for the encryption and decryption of data. Most widely used symmetric ciphers are AES and DES.

185.   **C** (Public Key Infrastructure)

Explanation: PKI is the combination of policies, procedures, hardware, software, and people that are required to create, manage and revoke digital certificates.

186.   **D** (When a VM that may have outdated security policies is brought online after a long period of inactivity)

Explanation: The condition Instant ON may create a potential danger to a VM when it is brought online after it has not been used for a long period of time because it may have outdated security policies and can introduce security vulnerabilities.

187.   **D** (Identify & Stops Malicious Traffic)

Explanation: SIO uses a monitoring database to differentiate legitimate traffic from malicious traffic to identify and prevent malicious traffic.

188.   **B** (Install antivirus scanner or software on all hosts)

Explanation: Anti-virus software is used to provide first layer of defense on end-user devices. It prevents malware from spreading. It generates automatic updates to ensure that hosts are protected from all kind of malwares.

189.   **D** (Financial gain)

Explanation:

Cyber criminals or attackers commonly attack or exploit data for money.

Hackers are known to hack for status.

Cyber-terrorists are motivated to commit cybercrimes for religious or political reasons.

190.   **B** (It authenticates a website and establishes a secure connection to exchange confidential data)

Explanation: Digital signatures rely on digital certificates to verify the identity of the originator in order to authenticate a vendor website and establish an encrypted

connection to exchange confidential data.

191. **D** (Asymmetric)

Explanation: An asymmetric encryption algorithm uses two keys, namely a public key and a private key. A symmetric encryption algorithm uses an identical key for both encryption and decryption. A shared secret is an example of using symmetric algorithm.

192. **B** (Shared Secret)

Explanation: A symmetric encryption algorithm uses an identical key for both encryption and decryption. A shared secret is an example of using symmetric algorithm.

193. **D** (Restricts unnecessary traffic from overloading the route processor)

Explanation: This plane involves the calculation of best routes in the network for traffic and filtering of data i.e. which packet to be sent to the next level or which packet to be discarded, device discovery and many more.

194. **D** (CLI view, Root view, Super view, Law intercept view)

Explanation: There are following types of role-based CLI access:

CLI view, Root view, Super view, Law intercept view.

195. **B** (1)

Explanation: By default, the Cisco IOS software command-line interface (CLI) has two levels of access to commands: User EXEC mode (level 1) and Privileged EXEC mode (level 15)

196. **C** (2)

Explanation:

To categorize the events, Syslog uses eight severity levels from zero to seven with zero being more critical one when system becomes severely degraded.

Emergencies	0	System is unusable
Alerts	1	Immediate Action needed
Critical	2	Critical Condition
Errors	3	Error Condition
Warnings	4	Warning Condition
Notifications	5	Normal but require attention

197.   **C** (SNMP)

Explanation: Simple Network Management Protocol (SNMP) is a protocol that provides the format of messages for communication between managers and agents. SNMP is an application layer protocol, which enables network administer to manage network heath, its performance and its problems.

198.   **A** (OIDs are organized in a hierarchical structure)

Explanation: MIB stands for Management Information Base and is a collection of information organized hierarchically in a virtual database.

199.   **B** (Authentication)

Explanation: Authentication is the process of proving an identity of a system by login identification and a password. It does the purpose of determining either the user is the same person he claims to be or not.

200.   **B** (TACACS)

Explanation: TACACS+ is also used as a communication between networking device and AAA server. Unlike RADIUS, TACACS+ encrypts the entire packet body, and also attaches TACACS+ header to the message body.

201.   **B** (SSH protocol has to be configured and a command must be issued to enable the SCP server side functionality)

Explanation: In order to configure Cisco device with SCP server's functionality, we first need to properly configure SSH and a username with proper authorization level for SCP to work properly. For authentication, a user must have a privilege level of 15. The command of "ip scp server enable" has to be issued to enable the SCP server side functionality.

202.   C (802.1x)

Explanation: The IEEE 802.1X authentication is an IEEE specification that is used to provide Port-based Network access control (PNAC) to the users. This specification is used to restrict unauthorized hosts from connecting to a LAN or WLAN. Each and every host that are intended to connect to the LAN must be authenticated to gain network access.

203.   B (BYOD)

Explanation: Bring your own device (BYOD) or bring you own technology (BYOT) refers to the network users who bring their own devices - such as smartphones, laptops and tablet PCs – for their work, they use them instead of company's given devices. It provides seamless connectivity between network and end users, while maintaining good security policies for an organization.

204.   C (MDM)

Explanation: Mobile Device Management (MDM) is a solution that provides a unified management of the entire network (mobile devices, smart phones, tablets, notebooks, Laptops etc.) from a centralized dashboard. The role of Mobile device managers is to manage, monitor and secure mobile devices of end users either they are organization's owned devices or employee-owned devices (BYOD).

205.   A (Enable Secret Password)

Explanation: AutoSecure executes a script that first makes recommendations for fixing security vulnerabilities and then modifies the security configuration of the router. AutoSecure can lock down the management plane functions and the forwarding plane services and functions of a router, and this includes setting an enable password, and a security banner.

206.   D, E, F (Create a view using the parser view view-name command, Assign a secret password to the view, Assign commands to the view)

Explanation: Here are the following steps involved in the creation of a view on cisco routers:

a) First of all, enable AAA.
b) Create a specific view.

c) Assign a secret password to that view.

d) Assign command to that view.

e) View configuration mode must be exited.

207.   **A, D, F** (Enable inbound vty SSH sessions, Configure IP domain name on the router, Generate SSH keys)

Explanation: Following are the steps to configure SSH on a cisco router:

a) Set the domain name.

b) Generate secret key.

c) Assign username and password.

d) Enable SSH inbound on a VTY lines.

208.   **B, C, D** (Specifies the database where captured information is stored, Gathers logging information, Compares the information to be captured and the information to be ignored)

Explanation: Syslog logging service includes, information gathering, evaluating which information to gather and which information to discard and leads the captured information to the storage devices. This information will stay in the storage device for a certain period of time, after that period all information will be vanished and will not be retained when a router is rebooted. It does not authenticate or decrypt messages.

209.   **A** (Data Plane)

Explanation: Data plane also known as user plane or forwarding plane. This plane involves the transaction of data packets. We apply policies over this layer to control user's traffic. Packets are sent and received through this part of a network so it takes care of packet flow, it is responsible for forwarding the traffic to the destination using information provided by other planes.

210.   **C** (Management Plane)

Explanation: Management plane involves the configuration, management and monitoring of networking devices. It involves accessing the CLI of any device, configuration of IP subnets, configuration of routing protocols and supporting protocols used to access the device. For example, using Telnet, SSH or console port to access router or switch etc. Similarly, when we use SNMP, Syslog, NTP to get information related to different nodes on a network, it is also a part of management plane.

211. **C** (Version 3)

Explanation: SNMP v3 Supports both encryption (DES) and hashing (MD5 or SHA). Implementation of version 3 has three models.

    a) NoAuthNoPriv means no encryption and hashing will be used.

    b) AuthNoPriv means only MD5 or SHA based hashing will be used.

    c) AuthPriv means both encryption and hashing will be used for SNMP traffic.

212. **B** (NTP)

Explanation: Network time protocol (NTP) is a protocol that allows networking devices like routers, switches etc. to synchronize their time with respect to the NTP server, so the devices may have more authenticated time settings and generated syslog messages can be observed more easily, and helps in analyzing problems and attacks during troubleshooting.

213. **B** (Control Plane)

Explanation: Inside the control function/plane lies any kind of traffic which requires some kind of processing usage of networking device. Control plane determines routing Protocols path calculation and their updates. Traffic directed to the IP address of Device itself.

214. **B** (Use the show aaa local user lockout command)

Explanation: The "show aaa local user lockout" command presents an administrator a list of the user accounts that are locked out and unable to be used for authentication. This command also provides the date and timestamp of the lockout occurrence.

215. **C** (Implement Cisco Secure Access Control System (ACS) only)

Explanation: Cisco Secure Access Control System (ACS) supports both RADIUS and TACACS servers. Local databases do not support these servers.

216. **E** (4)

Explanation:

To categorize the events, Syslog uses eight severity levels from zero to seven with zero being more critical one when system becomes severely degraded.

Emergencies	0	System is unusable
Alerts	1	Immediate Action needed
Critical	2	Critical Condition
Errors	3	Error Condition
Warnings	4	Warning Condition
Notifications	5	Normal but require attention

217.   **B** (NTP)

Explanation: In order to synchronize the time over, the *Network Time Protocol (NTP)* is used. NTP v3 being latest is used due to its support for encryption.

218.   **A** (VPN uses virtual connections to create a secure tunnel over a public network)

Explanation: VPN is a logical network that allows connectivity between two devices. That devices can either belongs to the same network or connected over a wide area network. The term "Virtual" here refers to the logical link between the two devices, as the VPN link does not exist separately, it uses internet as a transport mechanism. The term "Private" here refers to the security VPN provides to the connection between the two devices, as the medium of transport is internet, which is not secure and VPN adds confidentiality and data integrity.

219.   **A, C, D, E** (Confidentiality, Data integrity, Authentication, Anti-replay Protection)

Explanation: Following are the key features of VPN technology:

Confidentiality: Data is sent in an encrypted form, data for any other person would be meaningless.

Data integrity: VPN makes sure that the sent data is accurate, secure and remains unaltered end to end.

Authentication: VPN authenticate the peer on both side of the tunnel through pre shared public or private keys or by using user's authentication method.

Anti-replay Protection: VPN technology makes sure that if any VPN packet has sent for transaction and accounted for, then the exact same packet is not valid in the second time of VPN session, so no one can befool VPN peer into believing that the peer trying to connect is the real one.

220. **B** (Remote-access VPN)

Explanation: Types of VPN

a) Remote access VPN makes a networking device to connect outside a corporate office.

b) Site-to-site VPN connects two or more sites that want to connect together over the internet.

221. **A, B, D** (IPsec, SSL & MPLS)

Explanation: The three broad types of VPN technologies used today are:

a) **IPsec:** Used for connecting whole site with another site, IPsec provides security of IP packets at *Network Layer* of TCP/IP stack.

b) **SSL:** Supported by latest web browsers and custom-made software for clients, SSL encrypts TCP traffic by using encrypted SSL tunnels.

c) **MPLS:** *Multi-Protocol Label Switching (MPLS)* and *L3 MPLS VPN* are normally used by service providers to provide logical connectivity between two sites of an organization. IPsec is then used on top of L3 VPN connectivity to provide encryption.

222. **B** (IPsec)

Explanation: The main objective of IPsec is to provide CIA (confidentiality, integrity and authentication) for virtual networks used in current networking environments. IPsec makes sure the above objectives are in action by the time packet enters a VPN tunnel until it reaches the other end of tunnel.

223. **B, C, E** (AH, ISAKMP & ESP)

Explanation: ESP, AH, and ISAKMP must all be permitted through the perimeter routers and firewalls in order to establish IPsec site-to-site VPNs. NTP and HTTPS are application protocols and are not required for IPsec.

224. **C** (During both Phase 1 and 2)

Explanation: An IPsec VPN connection creates two SAs:

a) First at the completion of the IKE Phase 1 once the peers negotiate the IKE SA policy

b) Second at the end of IKE Phase 2 after the transformed sets are negotiated.

225.   C (Negotiation of IPsec policy)

Explanation: An IPsec VPN connection creates two SAs:

a) First at the completion of the IKE Phase 1 once the peers negotiate the IKE SA policy

b) Second at the end of IKE Phase 2 after the transformed sets are negotiated.

226.   A, B (AH provides integrity and authentication, ESP provides encryption, authentication, and integrity)

Explanation: There are two primary protocols used with IPsec are AH and ESP:

a) AH is protocol number 51 and provides data authentication and integrity for IP packets that are exchanged between the peers.

b) ESP, which is protocol number 50, performs packet encryption.

227.   C, E (MD5 & SHA)

Explanation: IPSec uses SHA, HMAC and MD5 authentication algorithm in tunnel mode for data integrity and authentication.

228.   C, E (51 & 50)

Explanation: There are two primary protocols used with IPsec are AH and ESP:

c) AH is protocol number 51 and provides data authentication and integrity for IP packets that are exchanged between the peers.

d) ESP, which is protocol number 50, performs packet encryption.

229.   B (The VPN connection is initiated by the remote user)

Explanation: A remote access VPN makes a networking device to connect outside a corporate office. These devices include smartphones, tablets, laptops etc. commonly known as end devices.

For example, a user wants to build a VPN connection from his individual computer to the corporate headquarters or any other branch of an organization. This is referred to as a remote-access VPN connection.

230. **B** (Transport mode)

Explanation: In transport mode, IPSec VPN secures the data field or payload of originating IP traffic by using encryption, hashing or both. New IPSec headers encapsulate only payload field while the original IP headers remain unchanged. Tunnel mode is used when original IP packets are source and destination address of secure IPSec peers.

231. **C** (MPLS)

Explanation: Multiprotocol Label Switching (MPLS) and MPLS Layer 3 VPNs are the VPN services provided by the internet service provider to allow an organization with two or more branches to have logical connectivity between the sites using the service provider's network for transport. This is also a type of VPN and called MPLS L3VPN, but it does not provide any encryption by default.

232. **B** (Allows NAT to work transparently on one or both ends of the VPN connection)

Explanation: NAT-Traversal encapsulates the datagram with a UDP packet. By doing so, source and destination ports along with source and destination IP addresses will also be included inside a new packet and NATing will work successfully in this case.

233. **C** (Hairpinning)

Explanation: Hair-pinning is a method where a packet goes out from an interface but instead of moving towards the internet it makes a hair pin turn, and returns back to the same interface.

234. **C** (DES)

Explanation:

a) Algorithms that are used to ensure that data is not intercepted and altered (data integrity) are MD5 and SHA.

b) AES and DES are common encryption protocol and provides data confidentiality.

c) DH (Diffie-Hellman) is an algorithm that is used for key exchange.

d) RSA is an algorithm used for authentication.

235. **D** (crypto ipsec transform-set ESP-DES-SHA esp-aes-256 esp-sha-hmac)

Explanation: DES uses 56-bit keys. 3DES uses 56-bit keys and encrypts three times which increases the overall encryption. AES uses 128-bit keys. AES-256 uses 256-bit keys, which is the strongest.

236. **C** (Allows peers to exchange shared keys)

Explanation: DH (Diffie-Hellman) is an algorithm used for key exchange. DH is a public key exchange method that allows two IPsec peers to establish a shared secret key over an insecure channel.

237. **B** (MD5)

Explanation:

a) Algorithms that are used to ensure that data is not intercepted and altered (data integrity) are MD5 and SHA.

b) AES and DES are common encryption protocol and provide data confidentiality.

238. **B, C** (area 0 authentication message-digest, ip ospf message-digest-key 1 md5 IPSpecialist)

Explanation: First command shown above defines the authentication type to be message digest. In the second command, authentication password is defined.

239. **A** (To configure OSPF MD5 authentication globally on the router)

Explanation: By using MD5 for hashing, route updates along with other routing information will not be in clear text format and hence enhance the overall security posture of network to some extent.

240. **C** (A snapshot of running configuration of the router can be taken and securely archived in a storage device.)

Explanation: Cisco IOS has a great feature of *"resilient configuration"*, which makes a backup copy running IOS image and configuration to mitigate the accidental or malicious attempts of erasing flash and NVRAM of devices.

241. **B** (Shows the list OSPF neighbors)

Explanation: The show "ip ospf neighbor" command observes the neighbor's data structure.

242. **C** (Cisco Express Forwarding (CEF))

Explanation: *Cisco Express Forwarding (CEF)* is the default option selected for the control plane's working mechanism. In CEF, switching cache makes the route for the session in advance even before any packets need to be processed.

243. **A, C** (Forwarding Information Base (FIB) & Adjacency Table)

Explanation: CEF uses two main components to perform its function: The **Forwarding Information Base (FIB)** and the **Adjacency Table**. The FIB makes the forwarding decision for the destination of the packet. It contains information like next hops, prefixes and the outgoing interfaces. The Adjacency Table carries the information about the next directly connected hops.

244. **D** (Restricts unnecessary traffic from overloading the route processor)

Explanation: Control Plane Policing (CoPP) is implemented, which identify specific traffic type and limits its rate that is reaching the control plane of the device.

245. **E** (All)

Explanation: Here is the list of Common Layer 2 attacks discussed in our workbook:

STP attacks, ARP spoofing, MAC spoofing, CAM table (MAC address table) overflows, CDP/LLDP reconnaissance, VLAN hopping and DHCP spoofing.

246. **B** (ARP Spoofing)

Explanation: ARP spoofing is a type of attack in which an attacker actively listens for ARP broadcasts and sends its own MAC address for given IP address. Now, if an attacker provides its MAC address against the IP address of default gateway of LAN, then man-in-the-middle attack will be easily launched without much effort.

247. **B** (MAC Spoofing)

Explanation: MAC Spoofing is a technique of manipulating MAC address to impersonate the legitimate user or launch attack such as Denial-of-Service attack. As we know, MAC address is built-in on Network interface controller, which cannot be changed, but some drivers allow to change the MAC address. This masking process of MAC address is known as MAC Spoofing.

248.   **C** (DHCP Snooping)

Explanation: DHCP snooping validates the DHCP messages received from either the legitimate source or from an untrusted source and filters out invalid messages. It is actually very easy for someone to bring accidentally or maliciously a DHCP server in a corporate environment. *DHCP snooping* is all about protecting against it.

249.   **D** (All of the above)

Explanation: Here is the list **of** Mitigation procedures of layer 2 attacks:

DHCP snooping, Dynamic ARP Inspection, port security, BPDU guard, root guard, loop guard.

250.   **B** (Loop Guard)

Explanation: Loop Guard feature helps you to prevent loop creation after STP is converged and redundant links are disabled. It prevents root ports or alternate ports from becoming designated ports in case of failure it leads towards unidirectional link. This feature is applicable to all the ports that are or can be non-designated.

251.   **A** (It binds the MAC address of known devices to the physical port and associates it with violation action)

Explanation: Port Security is used to bind the MAC address of known devices to the physical ports and violation action is also defined.

252.   **D** (Shows clients list with the legitimate IP addresses assigned to them)

Explanation: *"show ip dhcp snooping binding"* command can be used to display client lists with legitimate IP addresses assigned to them.

253.   **D** (DHCP Starvation)

Explanation: DHCP Starvation attack is a Denial-of-Service attack on DHCP server. In

DHCP Starvation attack, Attacker sends bogus requests for broadcasting to DHCP server with spoofed MAC addresses to lease all IP addresses in DHCP address pool. Once, all IP addresses are allocated, upcoming users will be unable to obtain an IP address or renew the lease.

254.   A, C, E (Disable auto-trunking and enable manual-trunking, Change the native VLAN to a VLAN other than VLAN1, Tag the native VLAN traffic in order to prevent against 802.1Q double-tagging attack to exploit network vulnerability)

Explanation:

Here are some precautionary measures to overcome VLAN hopping:

a) Disable trunking on all access ports.

b) Disable auto-trunking and enable manual-trunking.

c) Change the native VLAN to a VLAN other than VLAN1.

d) Tag the native VLAN traffic in order to prevent against 802.1Q double-tagging attack to exploit network vulnerability.

255.   **B** (If there is an attempt to write more data to a memory location than that location can hold)

Explanation: By sending too much data to a specific area of memory, adjacent memory locations are overwritten, which causes a security issue because the program in the overwritten memory location is affected.

256.   **C** (VLAN double-tagging)

Explanation: In a VLAN double tagging attack, an attacker can Spoof DTP messages from the attacking host to cause the switch to enter trunking mode. Here, he applies double tagging the first tag comprises of native VLAN to bypass trunking and other tag is of victim's VLAN to reach the victim. So that, the attacker can send traffic tagged with the target VLAN, and the switch simply delivers the packets to the destination. So it is better to configure any other VLAN as native VLA rather than VLAN 1.

257.   **B** (DTP)

Explanation: We can mitigate a VLAN hopping attack by disabling Dynamic Trunking Protocol (DTP) and by setting the native VLAN of trunk links to a VLAN not

in use.

258.   **B** (On a promiscuous port)

Explanation: Here are the following modes of Private VLAN:

a) **Promiscuous Mode:** Normally connected to a router, this port is allowed to send and receive frames form any other port on the same VLAN.

b) **Isolated Mode:** As name suggests, devices connected to isolated ports will only communicate with Promiscuous ports.

c) **Community Mode:** Community mode is used for group of users who want communication between them. Community ports can communicate with other community port members and with Promiscuous ports.

259.   **D** (Port security)

Explanation: Port security feature allows limited number of MAC addresses on a single port. So, if an attacker tries to connect its PC or embedded device to the switch port, then it will shut down or restrict the attacker from even generating an attack.

260.   **A** (It prevents rogue switches from being part of a network)

Explanation: BPDU guard feature error-disables a port that receives a BPDU. This prevents rogue switches from being a part of the network.

261.   **A** (clientless SSL)

Explanation: When a web browser is used to securely access the corporate network, the browser must use a secure version of HTTP to provide SSL encryption. A VPN client is not required to be installed on the remote host, so a clientless SSL connection is used.

262.   **D** (Both SSL and IPsec)

Explanation: Both IPsec and SSL are supported by Cisco AnyConnect.

263.   **B, C, D** (It has the ability to inspect the traffic of more than just IP and port level, By integrating with AAA, firewall can permit or deny traffic based on AAA policy, By integrating with IPS/ID, firewall can detect and filter malicious data at the edge of network to protect the end-users.)

Explanation: Firewalls are physical devices and software that defend an internal network or system from unauthorized access by using the traffic-filtering feature.

a) Firewall hides the functionality of network devices, which makes it difficult for an attacker to understand the physical topology of network.

b) It has the ability to inspect the traffic more than just IP and port level.

c) By integrating with AAA, firewall can permit or deny traffic based on AAA policy.

d) By integrating with IPS/ID, firewall can detect and filter malicious data at the edge of network to protect the end-users.

264.   **B** (Application-Level Firewall)

Explanation: Application level firewalls can operate up to layer 7 and provides a more granular control of packets moving in and out of network. Similarly, it becomes very difficult for an attacker to get the topology view of inside or trusted network because connection requests terminate on Application/Proxy firewalls.

265.   **A** (Circuit-Level Firewall)

Explanation: Circuit Level gateway firewall operates at the session layer of the OSI model. They capture the packet to monitor TCP Handshaking, in order to validate if the sessions are legitimate. Packets forwarded to the remote destination through a circuit-level firewall appear to have originated from the gateway.

266.   **D** (It provides better performance.)

Explanation: Both Stateful firewall and a proxy server do packet filtration but a Stateful firewall performs better than a proxy server. A Stateful firewall cannot authenticate users or prevent Layer 7 attacks.

267.   **A** (It is not as effective with UDP- or ICMP-based traffic.)

Explanation: Here are some limitations of Stateful firewalls:

• Stateful firewalls cannot prevent application layer attacks.

• Protocols such as UDP and ICMP are not Stateful and do not generate information needed for a state table.

• An entire range of ports must sometimes be opened in order to support specific

applications that open multiple ports.

- Stateful firewalls lack user authentication.

268. D (Establishes policies between zones.)

Explanation: Here are the following steps to configure zones in a Zone-based policy firewall:

a) Determine the zones.

b) Establish policies between zones.

c) Design the physical infrastructure.

d) Identify subnets with zones and see traffic requirements.

269. D (Stateful Firewall)

Explanation: Stateful firewalls analyze the state of connections in data flows during packet filtering. They analyze whether the packet belongs to an existing flow of data or not.

270. C (show running-config)

Explanation: The below command can verify zone based policy firewalls:

Show running-config, show zone security and show zone-pair security.

271. D (It saves the state of current sessions in a table)

Explanation: When the first packet from source hits the trusted interface of ASA, its entry will be made in Stateful database. As its name depicts, this saves the state of current sessions in a table known as Stateful database. This database is also called state table or session table. The incoming traffic of connection will only be allowed if source address and port number matches the saved state in the Stateful table.

272. B (Inside Global)

Explanation: Following table summarizes the different terminologies of NAT/PAT.

Inside Local	The original IP address of host from trusted network. For example 172.16.0.5 has been assigned to end users in diagram above
Inside Global	The global address either router's interface IP or one from pool, which will represent the client out on the internet.
Outside Local	The IP address with which a device is known on the internet. For example, the IP cameras, which are configured to be accessed anywhere from the internet.
Outside Global	The real IP address of host device, which is configured to be accessed over the internet. Like the private IP address of IP camera, which will be accessed via some global IP address.

273. **B** (Class map)

Explanation: Class maps are used to filter out the traffic that needs to be inspected. Traffic can be filtered by using information from Layer 3 up to Layer 7 of OSI model. ACL can also be referred in a class map for the purpose of identifying traffic.

274. **A** (Policy map)

Explanation: Policy maps are used to perform a specific kind of action on traffic matched by class maps. By referring a class-map, policy map can either inspect (Stateful inspection of traffic), permit (permit the traffic but no Stateful inspection), drop the traffic or generate log of it.

275. **A, B, E** (Drop, Permit, Inspect)

Explanation: Policy map can either inspect (Stateful inspection of traffic), permit (permit the traffic but no Stateful inspection), drop the traffic or generate log of it.

276. **B, C, D** (Command Line Interface (CLI), ASA Security Device Manager (ASDMo), Cisco Security Manager (CSM))

Explanation: Following are the official management techniques for accessing ASA firewall:

a) **Command Line Interface (CLI):** With a little bit change, most feature and syntax for basic operation is same as Cisco IOS of routers and switches, etc.

b) **ASA Security Device Manager (ASDM):** Just like Cisco Configuration

Professional (CCP), which is used to manage routers via GUI, ASDM is used to manage ASA in the same way.

c) **Cisco Security Manager (CSM):** A GUI based tool, which can be used to manage the network devices like routers, switches and security devices like firewalls.

277. **B** (Pass)

Explanation: The pass action in a Cisco IOS Zone-Based Policy Firewall is similar to a permit statement in an ACL.

278. **B** (Forwards traffic from one zone to another)

Explanation: The pass or permit action performed by Cisco IOS ZPF permits the traffic without Stateful inspection.

279. **B** (Transparent Mode)

Explanation: In transparent mode, ASA works as layer 2 bridge and traffic flows through it without adding itself as routing hop between communicating peers. Consider it as a tap on a network, which is normally used to analyze the network traffic.

280. **A** (Routed Mode)

Explanation: Usually, Cisco's ASA supports two firewall modes:

Routed mode

By default, Cisco ASA works in layer 3 or routed mode in which an IP address is normally assigned to different interfaces of the device. End-hosts see firewall as a routing hop along with the network path.

Transparent mode

In transparent mode, ASA works as layer 2 bridge and traffic flows through it without adding itself as routing hop between communicating peers. Consider it as a tap on a network, which is normally used to analyze the network traffic

281. **A** (Active/Standby failover)

Explanation: In Active/Standby failover, one device will act as primary firewall or active firewall while the second one will be in standby mode. Just like HSRP, the

standard protocol traffic will be exchanged periodically between firewalls to check the status of active and standby firewalls.

282.   A (Context)

Explanation: High-end ASA devices allow you to make multiple virtual firewalls within single hardware device. These virtual firewalls are known as context. Instead of using single hardware firewall for each client connection, service providers can use one high-end firewall and create multiple contexts in it.

283.   A (On inside interface)

Explanation: Security level 100- By default, it is used by the inside interface. It is the highest possible and the most trusted level.

284.   A (Security Access Policy)

Explanation: Security access policies specify the rules for the data traffic passing through an interface. These policies will be applied first, before any other policy to the incoming or outgoing traffic. Each packet that hits the interface will be first examined to decide whether to forward or drop the packet based on the criteria you specify in the access policy.

285.   A (AES)

Explanation: Data confidentiality can be implemented through symmetric encryption algorithms, including DES, 3DES, and AES.

286.   A (Two public keys are used for the key exchange.)

Explanation: An asymmetric encryption algorithm uses two keys, namely a Public Key and a Private Key.

287.   B (56-bits)

Explanation: DES uses a fixed length of key of 64-bits long, but only 56 bits are used for encryption. Rest of the bits is parity bits.

288.   B (Zero-Day Attack)

Explanation: A **zero-day attack** or zero-day threat is an attack that exploits the

weakness of any software that are unknown by the software vendor. An attacker can launch attack before the vendor releases any patch of this vulnerability and the network can be compromised.

289.   **B, C** (Both mitigate the network attacks either actively or passively, both are deployed as sensors)

Explanation: IDS and the IPS are deployed as sensors and use digital signatures to detect malicious traffic. IDS relies on an IPS to stop malicious traffic.

290.   **D, E** (The IDS requires other devices to respond to attacks, The IDS does not stop malicious traffic)

Explanation: IDS works passively, as it works on the copied traffic so IDS cannot stop or respond to an attack. IDS works in assistance with other devices like routers and firewalls to react against such attacks.

291.   **D** (All of the above)

Explanation: An IDS/IPS sensor could be placed in-line between any of the zones i.e. Inside, Outside or DMZ and the firewall.

292.   **D** (Network-based IPS cannot analyze encrypted traffic)

Explanation: Network-based IPS devices are implemented as inline mode to actively monitor the traffic on networks. They can take immediate actions when security policy breaches. One limitation of network based IPS is that they cannot monitor/inspect encrypted packets.

293.   **B** (False Positive)

Explanation: A false positive is a situation when sensor generates an alert about the traffic, which is not malicious, but requires serious attention as long as security is concerned. False positive can be easily identified, as immediate alerts are generated for this and they can be easily viewed.

294.   **D** (True Positive)

Explanation: A true positive means that a malicious activity is detected by the IPS module or sensor and an alert will be generated for this. Depending on the

configuration of IPS, it may be dropped at the first place.

295. D (All of the above)

Explanation: The following table summarizes the different technologies used in IDS/IPS along with its uses:

Signature Based	Easier Implementation and management.
Anomaly Based	It can deny any kind of latest attacks, as they will not be defined within the scope of baseline policy.
Policy Based	Everything else outside the scope of defined policy will be dropped.
Reputation Based	Uses the information provided by Cisco Could Services in which systems share their experience with network attacks.

296. B (To collect the information from the systems participating in global correlation and filters out sites or URLs with bad reputation)

Explanation: The role of Reputation based IDS/IPS is to collect the information from the systems participating in global correlation. Reputation based IDS/IPS include relative descriptors like known URLs, domain-names etc. Global correlation services are maintained by Cisco Cloud Services. So, it would be feasible to filter out the known traffic, which results in propagation of any attack.

297. B, D (Alert, Monitor)

Explanation: Here are some following terms, that define actions or responses that are commonly used in IDS technology:

a) **Alerts:** It is a generation of loggable messages upon every detection of malware or malicious traffic flows. The term "alarm" is also used for this purpose.

b) **Monitor:** An IDS can only monitor and analyze traffic, as it could not prevent an attack from reaching its destination but it can respond to a suspicious event with the help of other resources like routers and firewalls.

298. E (All of the above)

Explanation: Now here are some following terms, that define actions or responses that are commonly used in IPS technology:

a) **Drop:** It prevents the suspicious payload from reaching the destination.

b) **Reset:** Whenever the sensor detects a suspicious payload with a TCP

connection, the sensor will inject TCP resets, which leads to the termination of that particular TCP connection.

c) **Block:** IPS uses "block" action to ignore suspicious traffic coming from other protocols rather than TCP.

d) **Shun:** If IPS wants the above action of blocking to be performed by some other device like SIEM, then this dynamic action of blocking is referred to as Shunning.

299. **A** (Atomic)

Explanation: Here are some following micro engines for signature:

Atomic	Signatures designed to analyze single packets instead of stream of packets.
Service	Signatures designed to analyze application layer services.
String or multistring	This category contains signatures, which can compare and match custom patterns inside a single or stream of packets.
Other	Remaining signatures, which may not fit in the above categories.

300. **C** (Attack Severity Rating (ASR))

Explanation:

Attack Severity Rating (ASR)	It is also the part of digital signature and it determines the critical level of an attack.

301. **B** (It cannot detect unknown attacks)

Explanation: Signature or pattern based IDS/IPS only mitigates already discovered attacks. It compares the network traffic to a database of known attacks. Hence, this type of intrusion detection cannot detect unknown attacks. It is easy to configure and deploy.

302. **B** (Event correlation)

Explanation: Global correlation services are maintained by Cisco Cloud Services. It makes the network feasible to filter out the known traffic, which results in propagation of any attacks before it hits the organization's critical infrastructure.

303. **A** (Promiscuous or passive mode)

Explanation: In a promiscuous or passive mode, a copy of every data packet will be

send to the sensor to analyze any malicious activity. The sensor, running in promiscuous mode will perform the detection and generate an alert if required.

304.   **B** ('fail-open' mode)

Explanation: If 'fail-open' mode is used, the good and malicious traffic will be allowed in case of any kind of failure within IPS sensor.

If 'fail-close' mode is configured, the whole IP traffic will be dropped in case of sensor's failure.

305.   **B** (Dynamic Blacklist)

Explanation: IPS helps you to dynamically create a blacklist, with the help of Cisco Collective Security Intelligence Team "Talos" (http://www.talosintel.com/).

It dynamically downloads a collection of IP addresses at regular intervals that have a poor reputation in a networking environment.

306.   **B** (Whitelisting)

Explanation: Whitelisting is just the opposite of blacklisting, here you allow or permit IP address or traffic of your own choice.

Blacklisting and whitelisting are widely used for security solutions, including IPS, web security, E-mail security, and firewall.

307.   **B** (IPS does not responds immediately to an attack)

Explanation: IPS responds immediately to an attack and does not allow any malicious traffic to bypass network device, but it introduces delay in a network as it analyzes each and every packet that passes through an interface.

308.   **D** (All of the above)

Explanation: IPS provides network protection by preventing an attack to reach its destination, by enforcing policies, by controlling access to resources and by hardening networking devices.

309.   **D** (All of the above)

Explanation: Here are some common types of E-mail based threats found in today's networks are:

a) **Spam:** A spam can be an E-mail with malicious content. It can be categorized based on its subject or files attached to the E-mail, etc.

b) **Malware Attachments:** Any kind of malware or malicious executed program, attached to an E-mail.

c) **Phishing:** It tries to get login credentials by manipulating the end-user by presenting different links, which looks legitimate, for example presenting fake social web pages.

310.   **A** (Phishing attack)

Explanation: Phishing tries to get login credentials by manipulating the end-user by presenting different links, which looks legitimate, for example presenting fake social web pages.

311. **B, C, E** (E-mail Encryption, Network Anti-virus, Access Control)

Explanation: Following are the few features provided by AsyncOS running on ESA devices:

a) **Access Control:** Just like *Access-List,* access control provides inbound control by using either sender's IP address/subnet or domain name.

b) **Anti-spam:** Powered by Cisco research group *Talos,* anti-spam is a multilayer protection filter based on Cisco SenderBase Reputation feature.

c) **Network Antivirus:** Partnership with Sophos and MacAfee® for integration of their scanning engines allow anti-virus scanning capabilities at the edge of network.

d) **AMP and DLP features:** Data Loss Prevention (DLP) helps to prevent any critical digital asset from leaving the corporate network by monitoring the outbound traffic. Similarly, AMP feature helps to mitigate against latest threats and attacks.

e) **E-mail Encryption:** The network management team can utilize the encryption feature for outbound E-mails.

f) **E-mail Authentication:** *ESA* can use multiple authentication mechanism to verify the authenticity of coming E-mails.

g) **Outbreak Filters:** This feature provides mitigation against latest security outbreaks by using Cisco's threat intelligence information.

312.   **D** (All of the above)

Explanation: The features of Cisco AMP include the followings:

a) **File reputation:** Here the malicious traffic will automatically be blocked. File reputation service is updated after every 3 to 5 minutes.

b) **File sandboxing:** It gathers details about a file's behavior to determine the file's threat level and it sends the results to Cisco cloud based intelligence service named as TALOS, which then updates the treat and its mitigations globally.

c) **File retrospection:** It analyzes and solves the problem of malicious files that pass through the email security gateway but might later cause a threat.

313.**B** (File sandboxing)

Explanation: File sandboxing analyzes unknown files that are traversing the Cisco E-mail security gateway. It gathers details about a file's behavior to determine the file's threat level and it sends the results to Cisco cloud based intelligence service named as TALOS, which then updates the treat and its mitigations globally.

314.   **B** (Context-Based Filtering)

Explanation: Content based filtering inspects the entire mail, including message contents, analyzing details such as sender identity, its source, its destination, embedded URLs, attachments and E-mail formatting by using algorithms. It identifies spam messages without blocking the legitimate E-mail.

315.   **C** (Anti-Malware Protection(AMP))

Explanation: Cisco Advanced Malware Protection (AMP) provides control over malware detection and blocking. It provides continuous analysis of data to detect, analyze, track, confirm and mitigate threats before, during and after an attack.

316.   **B** (Deep content analysis)

Explanation: In case of E-mail security, Data Loss Prevention (DLP) is a content level scanning of messages and attachments in an E-mail, to detect whether the transport for sensitive data is appropriate or not.

317.   **A** (Pretty Good Privacy (PGP))

Explanation: OpenPGP is the most widely used E-mail encryption standard. The main purpose of OpenPGP is to ensure an end-to-end encryption over E-mail communication; it also provides message encryption and decryption and password manager, data compression and digital signing.

318.   **B** (URL Categorization)

Explanation: URL Categorization controls the user access to specific website category. This feature enables networking device to filter web traffic by using a categorization database.

319.   **C** (Web Application Filtering)

Explanation: Web application filtering protects your web or mobile applications from being compromised and prevents data from breaching. Web application filtering can be done by either defining filtering policy or by using web application firewall (WAF).

320.   **A, B, C** (It defines the rules and policies to allow or block specific application or data, it blocks hidden malware in encrypted SSL/TLS traffic, It detects and blocks intrusion attempts from an attacker)

Explanation: TLS/SSL decryption performs the following actions:

a) It blocks hidden malware in encrypted SSL/TLS traffic

b) It detects and blocks intrusion attempts from an attacker

c) It restricts confidential data from loss, hence provides Data Loss Prevention (DLP)

d) It defines the rules and policies to allow or block specific application or data

e) It monitors outgoing data

321.   **A, B, C** (Web Application Firewall (WAF), Cloud Based Web Security (CWS), Cisco Web Security Appliance(WSA))

Explanation:

a) **Cloud based Web Security:** Organizations having Cisco's cloud based web security gets their web access being monitored and scanned for any kind of threat.

b) **Web Security appliance (WSA):** WSA provides protection before, during and after an attack.

c) **Web application filtering:** Web application filtering protects your web or mobile applications from being compromised and prevents data from breaching.

322.   **B** (Cisco C370)

Explanation: The following table summarizes different variants of ESA series:

Cisco X1070	Service providers and large scale enterprise environment.
Cisco C680	Service providers and large scale enterprise environment.
Cisco C670	Medium sized enterprise environment.
Cisco C380	Medium sized enterprise environment.
Cisco C370	Small to medium sized enterprise environment.
Cisco C170	Small Office/Home Office (SOHO) environment.

323.   **E** (All of the above)

Explanation: Web based attacks includes cross-site scripting (XSS), SQL injection, file inclusion, cross-site forgery etc.

324.   **B** (Data at rest)

Explanation:

Following are the few commercial as well as open source software programs, which can be used to encrypt the data at rest, for example the files and folders of workstation or mobile device etc.

   a) **TrueCrypt:** A free data encryption software for Windows, MAC and Linux based operating system.

   b) **AxCrypt:** Similar in functionality to *TrueCrypt* but only available for Windows based environment.

   c) **BitLocker:** Latest versions of Microsoft Windows has pre-installed BitLocker software program, which provides full disk encryption and some other features.

   d) **MAC OS X FileVault:** Just like BitLocker, it provides features of full disk encryption on MAC OS X based systems.

325.   **A, B, C** (Generic Routing Encapsulation (GRE), Multiprotocol Label Switching (MPLS) VPN, Internet Protocol Security (IPsec))

Explanation: Following are the different protocols, which can be used in VPN implementation:

   a) Point-to-Point Tunneling Protocol (PPTP)

b) Layer 2 Forwarding (L2F) Protocol

c) Layer 2 Tunneling Protocol (L2TP)

d) Generic Routing Encapsulation (GRE)

e) Multiprotocol Label Switching (MPLS) VPN

f) Internet Protocol Security (IPsec)

g) Secure Sockets Layer (SSL)

326.   **A** (Advanced Malware Protection (AMP))

Explanation: Personal firewalls and *HIPS* are getting obsolete due to more advanced software available in the market today. The Cisco AMP covers the majority of operating systems (Windows, MAC OS X and android) and uses advanced features like device and file trajectory to help network administrators analyze the complete attack scenario.

About Our Products

Other products from IPSpecialist LTD regarding Cisco technology are:

- CCNA Routing & Switching Technology Workbook
- CCNA Security Technology Workbook
- CCNA Service Provider Technology Workbook
- CCNA CyberOps SECFND Technology Workbook
- CCDA Technology Workbook
- CCDP Technology Workbook
- CCNP Security (SENSS) Technology Workbook
- CCNP Security (SIMOS) Technology Workbook
- CCNP Security (SITCS) Technology Workbook
- CCNP Security (SISAS) Technology Workbook
- CCNP Routing & Switching (Route) Technology Workbook
- CCNP Routing & Switching (Switch) Technology Workbook
- CCNP Routing & Switching (Troubleshoot) Technology Workbook

Upcoming products from IPSpecialist LTD regarding AWS technology are:

- CCNA CyberOps SECOPS Technology Workbook
- CCNA Wireless Technology Workbook

Note from the Author:

Reviews are gold to authors! If you have enjoyed this book and it helped you along certification, would you consider rating it and reviewing it?

Link to Product Page: